Guided by Love

A Minister's Thoughts on Love, Hope, and Justice

Reverend Rebecca M. Bryan

WINTER ISLAND PRESS

Published by Winter Island Press
Salem, Massachusetts
winterislandpress.com

ISBN: 979-8-9925945-1-5 (paperback)
ISBN: 979-8-9925945-3-9 (large print)
ISBN: 979-8-9925945-2-2 (eBook)

Cover design by Lance Hidy

WINTER ISLAND PRESS

This book is dedicated to Love.

Love that is real and ever present, that brings a community together and guides us on our way. We will never realize the unifying power of community until we give ourselves to it and decide to dedicate ourselves to its shared values.

This book is my story as told over several years to the people I have had the privilege to lead and the honor to love. Ours is a relationship born in times of change and challenges.

The church membership has grown continually, even as we lost a significant number of longtime members who have died over the last seven years.

We made our way through the pandemic, sheltered each other through good times and bad, and opened our doors to an Afghan family of eleven people who lived in our Parish Hall for two years and continue to be good friends today.

We've developed partnerships with other organizations and people who are working on the same issues of justice that we support with our time, volunteer hours, and money.

We sing, we laugh, and we gather.

As a diverse body of believers and nonbelievers, we find belonging in our shared promises to one another and our commitment to justice for all people, beings, and the Earth, and our covenant to acting as a welcoming and inclusive community.

For all of these reasons, and so many more, I am grateful. I hope that some of what we talk about each Sunday may be of interest to you. For my beautiful people at First Religious Society Unitarian Universalist, FRSUU, may these sermons serve as a memory and a beacon of these first seven years together.

With love,

Contents

Space for Stories

September 9, 2018

As chaplains, we wore plain clothes—unlike others in the hospital, we had no uniform. Others did have uniforms: the nurses wore blue, the doctors white, those who worked in food service wore green.

Hartford Hospital was a large hospital with a diverse patient population in terms of race, culture, and religion. I was an interfaith chaplain for twelve months as part of my seminary training. My role as a chaplain was to provide pastoral care and end of life support to patients, family, friends, and medical staff. Hospital protocol for chaplains was for us to wear plain clothes. The only identifying objects were our name tags and the pagers on our belts. The challenge with this approach was that without anything distinguishing me from a civilian, I was met with suspicion and concern as I entered people's hospital rooms. People had no idea that I was a chaplain. How would they?

During my third week in this role, I tried something—I began wearing a necklace with a cross on it which was visible from a hospital bed. It could have been any religious symbol; I just wanted some image that would help people to identify me as a chaplain. I hoped that this imagery would give people some sense of the story behind who I was so that they would quickly realize why I was walking into their rooms. I was amazed at how well it worked!

I chose a cross to wear knowing that the majority of people in this hospital were Latino and Catholic. It was a simple cross, given to me in my childhood. Even I was surprised that such a seemingly small symbol had such a profoundly positive effect on how people received me. People smiled as I walked into their rooms regardless of their personal religious or theological beliefs. I would walk into the rooms and find visitors sitting with the patient in the bed. I'm sure most of us have been in a hospital room with a loved one; it's a vulnerable time. With few exceptions, patients and their visitors looked at the small cross around my neck as I walked into the room, took a deep breath, and said, "Thank goodness you are here."

The relief at my arrival was not implying, "Thank goodness you are here because I believe what you believe." No. What people needed and wanted at that moment was someone who would sit with them and offer a supportive presence. As a minister I could do that. I also listened to their stories, held their hands if they wanted, and prayed with them when it was helpful. Sometimes my prayer would include specific wishes and concerns that the patient or family had requested. Usually, though, I would pray back to them the stories they had told me. To pray someone's story is to weave what one hears into a prayer: the joys, sorrows, fears, and memories. Use the prayer to bless these human experiences and make them sacred.

After listening to their remembrances and fears, I would pray:

May Carol know peace.

May Sam know that their family is here for them.

May Lee know that they are loved.

The stories people told were both unique and universal. Themes of fear, regret, and gratitude were often shared. I would weave the stories and hopes into one prayer after another.

The art and craft of storytelling is ancient. Margaret Atwood says that storytelling "...is built into the human plan. We come with it."[1]

Our stories give our lives meaning and help us to make sense of the world. Our stories and the meaning we make of them can help give us a sense of control, which, though an illusion, is something that humans need in small doses to feel secure.

In addition to meaning-making, stories help us to develop empathy. A 2014 study, published in the journal *Basic and Applied Psychology*, reported that, "reading fiction significantly increased empathy towards others, especially people that readers initially perceived as 'others,' including people of a different race, culture or religion."[2]

Stories combine the memories in our head and our hearts. Stories resonate with people in a way that is both particular and universal. A marketing study from the Stanford Graduate School of Business reports that people remember information weaved into a story up to twenty-two times more than facts alone.[3]

We all have stories. You have a story. This church has a story. Every person has many stories of their own life. None of us has a single story of our life.

We (FRSUU and I) have already begun creating our story and the creation will go on for a long time. It behooves us to know each other's stories and the history and tales of the church. As we learn each other's experiences, we can share our own. As we come to know one another, we realize how wrong our assumptions about other people can be and we are made richer from other people's stories. We learn more about ourselves too and begin to look anew at our own stories.

I ask you to reflect upon your stories and how Unitarian Universalism and this congregation have affected you. What about your stories do you want to change? What has lived out its time? What about your storyline do you want to develop more fully? What are you ready to bring out from hiding into the light? Where have you developed a single story about yourself, this place, or other people?

Making space for stories necessitates that we take the time to listen to one another with an open mind and heart. As listeners, our task is to understand others; in so doing, we will also learn more about ourselves. This kind of storytelling fosters genuine relationships and makes us less likely to form a single story about a culture or group of people. For example, just because you know one New England Yankee doesn't mean you know them all. Just because you have a relationship with one Black person doesn't mean you now understand Black people. When we do not respect the diversity of people, we are prone to develop a single story that helps us to classify groups and people and put them into categories.

In her TED talk, "The Danger of a Single Story," Chimamanda Ngozi Adichie talks about growing up in Nigeria and how some of the stories of her upbringing were singular. For example, as a young child, she was only exposed to British and American children's books. Thus, she carried the single story that children's books had to be about white people.

Adichie was also taught a single story about people with less means, or "poor people." The single story of poor people was essentially that they have less money, fewer resources, and therefore less happiness. The author learned differently from a family friend.

I was also taught that people with less means were less happy than people who had more money. This single story was torn apart for me when I went to Tanzania. While there, I looked into the eyes of young children who were wearing Nike t-shirts and sneakers too large for their feet, and I saw a joy that I had never seen in the eyes of the white, middle class American children that I knew.

The dangers of holding a single story about people, cultures, or experiences is that these single stories affect how we perceive and interact with the world. There are often single stories behind racism, misogyny, xenophobia, and homophobia. When we believe that Black people are...fill in the blank... we are living in a single story, and we cut ourselves off from the richness of diversity.

We also limit our self-understanding when we define *ourselves* from a single story. When we believe that we are only our childhood, only our career, our addiction, our recovery, our mistakes, or our accomplishments, we live disconnected from our dreams, and from others. We are all people with many stories. Our stories do not determine our inherent worth and dignity; that is God-given.

Each of us is spectacular, made up of complicated, contradictory, good, not-so-good, and everything-in-between stories. And so is everyone else.

We need to constantly remind ourselves that we never know the full story of anyone or anything and that we are not a single story ourselves. Chimamanda Ngozi Adichie promises us that "...when we realize that there is never a single story about any place, we regain a kind of paradise."[4]

Back to the story I shared at the beginning of this sermon about being a chaplain. I talked about wearing a cross in the hospital. You will see me wear a cross here at FRS at times. You will also see me wear a chalice necklace, like this one passed on to me by one of my dear mentors at her retirement. You will also see me wear a gold necklace that has a goddess perched upon a moon, and a pewter necklace with a goddess who sits inside of a chalice. On other days I may wear an Om sign, or a crystal tucked into a pendant. All of these symbols are part of my story. My theology, I'm sure like yours, is not a single story.

Some people have asked why I prefer to be called "Reverend Rebecca." That's a fair question, and clearly a twist in the story of ministers here at FRSUU. Yes, I do prefer that you call me Reverend or Rev. Rebecca, though, of course, I'll love you no matter what you call me.

There is a story.

I learned of the value of being called Reverend—particularly for women, ministers of color, and other historically marginalized people in our faith tradition—first from my colleagues, then from personal experience.

When the Universalist Church in West Hartford, Connecticut, was being served by two female ministers, they spoke to the congregation of the fact that, let's face it, women ministers are treated differently from our male counterparts, who, until more recent times have comprised the majority of our clergy. Female ministers, unlike men, do not automatically receive the recognition of their position. For example, we need to wear a robe when we preach, in contrast to white male ministers who can just as comfortably don sports jackets and ties with a stole and still be recognized and respected as ministers. We still live in a patriarchal society, though it is changing. Why would our congregations be any different than the rest of our society? One of the ways we make change is to intentionally do things that promote such change. This is also true with biases against female and other historically marginalized groups of ministers.

The Reverend Cheryl Walker, UU Minister, shares her story of coming to be called Reverend in the book *Centering: Navigating Race, Authenticity, and Power in Ministry*. Rev. Walker speaks of the importance of using her title in terms of her role in the interfaith community as well as within her congregations. She writes, "Calling one's minister by their first name is seen by many outside of the UU tradition as disrespectful."[5]

As partners in interfaith work, we must be able to pray or march alongside our colleagues as identified clergy.

Equally important are boundaries. You, and everyone who seeks a spiritual community, deserves a spiritual leader, not a friend. You need to know that you can call on me and that I will be there, whatever your age or circumstance.

I'll be there when you want to discuss your spiritual story and journey or when you need a listening ear, a visit in the hospital, or a poem read at your sacred occasion. I cannot be a friend to more than 400 members; however, I can, and will with great love, be your minister.

"The real reason we tell stories," writes Cody Delistraty, "is because we want to be part of a shared story."[6] We here at FRSUU are starting our shared story together. It is a story that has been going on for nearly 300 years. It is hundreds of stories, each as unique and important as the next, coming together into a tapestry of wisdom.

I invite us all to consciously be a part of our collective experiences and the story we are creating together. What part of your many stories do you hide for fear of what others may think, here or anywhere? What do you actually want from others that you have been afraid to ask for?

Bring your whole story, including your crosses and your OM signs. Ask us to treat you as you would like to be treated. I want to know your stories, as many as you want to share. Don't let anyone tell you that your stories are wrong or insignificant. Your stories, like you, are a precious, irreplaceable part of Life's story. May we tell and receive each other's stories and may we all grow more whole as a result.

Part One

Nature

1
Her Voice
December 4, 2022

What is the nature of your homeland? Tell me what she taught you when you were very young. Did you learn of resiliency from the dandelion making her way through the seemingly impenetrable city sidewalk? Did you find yourself surrounded by the majesty of mountains or the embrace of the sea? Did the river or stream inspire or comfort you, or were you left longing, sitting inside of a house, looking out at the great mystery all around you?

I am of the land of cornstalks, taller than a child, even in junior high school. A woman in training, finding herself comforted by the soft bed of pine needles, sheltered in the dark forest areas behind a house filled with anger. I am of the land that fed milking cows, with calves nestling up to their teats, a land of good and plenty.

Tell me of your homeland and what it taught you.

And then share with me, if you will, when you first learned of the danger she faced, this Earth of ours.

When did you realize her fate was perilous and not a guaranteed fact of existence? When did you stop exhaling and hold your breath, overwhelmed at the immensity of the damage humans have caused and the problems facing our planet and her creatures?

Were you taught that the Earth sings? That woodpeckers and sparrows have journeys of flight involving their hearts as well as their wings? Can you tell the difference between a wild animal's cry for safety and one appealing to a prospective mate? Did you know trees communicate more than meets the eye and flowers are filled with life spirit and medicine? Or were you taught, as I was, that humans are the quintessential aim of all existence and that the rest of creation is less than alive, if alive at all?

No one explicitly taught me the language of animacy, or the belief that there is a source of aliveness and "being," not only in people, but in all living things such as fish, trees, and the wind. There were some people who inspired this knowing and reverence in me. My father carried me backpacking through forests up and down the eastern seaboard, bought me a subscription to *Ranger Rick* magazine for Christmas, and never laughed at my dreams of saving the planet or helping animals. My father taught me the language of animacy. For that, I am ever grateful.

The language of animacy, in which all of creation has agency and life force, is ubiquitous among Indigenous people and their beliefs. Some white people mock this, and many romanticize it. It is time to realize its truth and to honor it. It is time to recognize and live in relationship with the Earth and our fellow creatures. It is time to stop objectifying, denying, and distancing ourselves from the reality of life force all around us.

I could have begun this month of worship with a ministry theme of Earth from an intellectual place, reciting facts, statistics, and scientific predictions, all of which are over-whelming and easily lead to dismay or denial as a way of coping with their enormity. I might have entered more gently and offered a list of dos and don'ts to help us respond to the climate emergency. Those things matter. The predictions are valid and sound. Everything we do, small and large, matters. We ought to be knowledgeable and change what we can in ourselves, our community, and the world.

However, I am neither a scientist nor an ecological expert. I am a mother, a theologian, and a minister. I am called to remind you that all the knowledge in the world will not change our ways if our hearts do not also change. In fact, a changed heart, be it broken, opened, or both, is the most assured way to engagement and change.

Our world is alive, friends. She is crying for us to be in rela-tionship with her. The best way to do this is to be and feel our connection to the Earth in our hearts and bodies. This means we feel her pain, are blessed by her gifts, and are awed by her beauty.

Franciscan priest Richard Rohr encourages all of us to spend time genuinely communing with a single part of nature. This might mean that we get down on our knees and be with a blade of grass. We see the dew twinkle in the early morning light and watch the chlorophyll rebound in green vibrancy when it rains. We laugh at how the grass lies flat under the weight of our crawling grandchild and bounces back as they crawl to the next spot.

Robin Wall Kimmerer encourages us to realize how the English language has been used to distance us from the animacy of creation. "Linguistic imperialism has always been a tool of colonization...which renders the beloved land as lifeless object, the forest as board feet of timber," she writes.[7] "In English, you're either a human or a thing."[8] Whereas in Potawatomi, Kimmerer's language of origin, the world is divided into animate and inanimate rather than male and female. In the Potawatomi language, everything is alive.

She invites us to connect with life beyond humans using pronouns rather than "it" when referring to animals and parts of nature. "It" objectifies and distances us from the living around us.

Kimmerer imagines using the pronoun "ki," which in the plural form is "kin." Thus, a beautiful blue heron taking off from the marsh is not an "it"; it is instead a *ki*. And the seals in the ocean are *kin*, rather than objects separate from our fate. Doing this, we can begin to live and relate to the world around us as though it were "a democracy of species, not a tyranny of one," to use Kimmerer's phrase.

When we live in relationship with the living Earth and her creatures, we are not alone. We are kin. We feel gratitude for her many gifts. We feel compassion for the pains being inflicted on life around us. We feel grief and anger, and we are called to do what we can to love and protect the living web of which we are a part, because it breaks our heart not to. That's where I need us to reside—in our hearts and our bodies, relating to creation in love and gratitude.

When Robin Wall Kimmerer began to write about the Thanksgiving Address, which we shared together this morning, she was concerned about appropriation. After all, she is a member of the Potawatomi Nation, not the Haudenosaunce or Iroquois Confederacy, who created the beautiful words. She approached Oren Lyons, an Onondaga Faithkeeper, about this. His reply is haunting. He said, "Of course you should share it. We've been waiting five hundred years for people to listen. If they'd understood the Thanksgiving then, we wouldn't be in this mess."[9]

Kimmerer goes on to invite us as the readers to imagine what it would be like to have our school children recite the Thanksgiving Address instead of the Pledge of Allegiance. With no mal intent to veterans who have served our country, she writes how her hopes extend beyond traditional white people's views of the Republic.

The boundaries of what I honor are bigger than the republic...

Let us pledge reciprocity with the living world...

If what we want for our people is patriotism, then let us inspire true love of country by invoking the land herself...

If we want to raise good leaders, let us remind our children of the eagle and the maple...

If what we aspire to is justice for all, then let it be justice for all of Creation.[10]

And so may we enter our month-long journey into a ministry theme of Earth. May this be but the beginning of a lifelong journey toward wholeness.

2
Space of a River
December 5, 2021

I might have missed it: the chance to reconnect with God, eternity, goodness.

My husband, Bart, and I had just arrived at the Grand Canyon and checked into our dormitory-style room. We walked into the modest, aging space, my partner pulling our canvas luggage and I carrying water and other snacks suitable for hiking.

I walked up to the screened window with its less-than-perfect glass behind it and paused. Leaning my forehead against the window, I felt the rest of my body begin to let go, sliding down the wall. I involuntarily fell to my knees. The canyon was so beautiful that it took my breath away.

"Are you alright? Should I still go get the rest of the luggage?" Bart asked as he quietly left the room. He already knew the answer. He knows me well, and he knows when I've been summoned.

My tears started as I surrendered to what was happening. The Grand Canyon swept before me in all her grandeur, even as I could see only a small portion of her 1,904 square miles. It had been 33 years since my only other trip to the canyon. It seemed her majestic presence had grown over the years, and yet, I knew it was I who had grown deeper.

I began speaking, talking with the canyon as though she were a wise woman, as I believe she is.

"So much has happened..." I said through my tears. "Babies, losses, addiction, degrees, achievements, and joy..." It felt so good to be back in her presence, palpable though separated by a long distance and a little glass.

I had spent many years largely forgetting about the interconnection between me and Life. I had been busy: raising children, dealing with adversity, and embracing change. I had been living and loving most of what went on in those years, as hard as it was to do so at times. And I had forgotten my connection to this beautiful space which reminded me of my goodness.

Thirty-three years is but a drop in the ocean in the life of a canyon, formed by the flow of a river over a timeline ranging from 4 to 70 million years ago. My life was, and is, part of that water droplet, as is yours.

Two weeks later, I was able to articulate what had happened during this spiritual and mystical experience. I had experienced the Holy, not studied it, debated it, or tried to define it or defend it. I had simply allowed myself to surrender to the beauty of the canyon and thus had been held.

I had allowed myself to stop and listen to my inner knowing when I felt the pull of the canyon from beyond the screen window in our small room. It was a moment not to be missed. Thank God I listened.

There are two other places on Earth where I experience transcendence and remember the interconnection we share with all of life: the lands of Tanzania, particularly Mount Kilimanjaro, and a small lake in Orleans, Massachusetts, where my grand-parents spent their final years. Both serve as tangible reminders of Truth. A mountain, a lake, and a canyon: All three call me home to Universal love and belonging.

Through all that happened, from when I was young and naiver, until now when I am older and aware of all I don't know, the Grand Canyon—a loving, beautiful, holding space—had been there waiting. I went away, but she never left.

The canyon's layers reveal truths in nature and of time gone by, which to me are expressions of God: truth, change, consistency, and space, each affected by the laws of nature and the choices humans make.

The poet David Whyte describes such moments of transcendence in his poem "Sometimes."[11]

> *Sometimes*
> *if you move carefully...*
> *breathing*
> *like the ones*
> *in the old stories,*
>
> *you come to a place*
> *whose only task*

is to trouble you
with tiny
but frightening requests,

conceived out of nowhere
but in this place
beginning to lead everywhere...

Requests to stop what
you are doing right now,
and...

to stop what you
are becoming
while you do it...

So much would have been lost to me had I not taken the time or made the space to listen to what my heart was telling me: "Stop. Kneel. Connect. Share your Soul's truth."

I would have lost access to a vital spiritual experience had I done what I often do: Be efficient, bring in the luggage, finish the proverbial to-do list. That I had to make space to experience the divine is not lost on me.

Space—whether it be in our physical surroundings, our schedules, or our minds—is necessary for the winds of change and the experiences of gratitude and inspiration. Creating space in our hearts, by dropping expectations and resentments and extending forgiveness to ourselves or others, makes room for love and joy.

Many of us avoid making space because we forget its gifts and fear what we may find there. Space, my friends, literally and metaphorically, can feel scary and even overwhelming, and it is certainly not championed by mainstream culture. And yet, the most intimate, revelatory, healing, and necessary encounters generally require space.

The poet John O'Donohue reminds us that the absence encountered in space is not lifeless, rather it is "alive with hidden presence..." where "nothing is ever lost or forgotten."[12]

Spaciousness is relevant at any time of year. Consider spaciousness in the winter months, when space in the night sky is most visible. Dark night skies on cold winter nights remind us to look up, to see the stars, and connect to the truth that we are part of the Universal Story, both in its tragedies and its joys and mystery.

We belong, my friends, not only to ourselves and each other, but to this Earth, to life, and to death. We are part of the Mystery whether we remember it or not. In that moment at the Grand Canyon, I knew I was part of the Mystery and knowing that made all the difference.

May you create space in your life and may you find a way to meet its presence.

3
Come, Sunday
October 23, 2022

Monday morning is usually one of my favorite times of the week: my day off when I can spend time with my beloved equine friends—horses, donkeys, and mules. The animals I volunteer with are all living in an equine sanctuary, a safe environment filled with proper medical care and friendly care-givers. The attention and care support the animals in their recovery from various difficulties including mistreatment, neglect, and abandonment, while waiting to find their next "forever home."

This particular Monday, however, I didn't want to go to my volunteer commitment. It had been a long time since I had a sleep-in Monday. My husband and I had gotten COVID boosters the night before. I had hoped I might just feel "bad enough" that I could call off my volunteer duties that morning.

I wasn't feeling well and easily could have justified staying home with a warm cup of tea, but something got me out the door. As I now understand it, an act of grace had me pull on barn boots and gloves and head over to the farm.

Once there, I fell into my typical routine and nearly forgot that I almost hadn't come. Everything was normal, until I got over to the right-hand side of the pastures, where I immediately sensed something was awry. My footsteps slowed, almost of their own accord. I paused, buckets of grain in hand. Something was different.

The air was still. Nothing was moving. The animals, normally precocious, offered me none of their customary neighing and braying, expressing their eagerness to have their breakfast. Looking around, I saw every animal had their head hung low.

I opened the gate to the paddock, home to the miniature donkeys, only to find that one had died in the night. Its pocket-size body lay waiting to be found. I immediately realized that all of the animals knew, even the sheep. Their heads hung out of respect.

I knelt next to the animal and called the owner of the farm. As I waited for her to come, I suddenly realized this donkey's mate was nowhere in sight. I went into the small shelter in the paddock and found the other miniature donkey standing in the back of the shed, shaking.

I later learned that she was the mother of the one who had died. I spent hours with her that morning, just holding her head as she leaned into my lap, resting all her weight on my body. We prayed. We walked. We stopped. We cried and we loved. Just like any two people would do. I was honored and in awe to be with her during this time, and my heart ached for her. There is no separation between God's creations.

I later learned that her name was Sunday. In the days to come, volunteers rallied around her, spending time with her and walking her. She didn't want to eat, so we fed her molasses in chopped hay—making it taste sweet and stick to her bones. We weren't sure if she would pull out of her grief, and we felt powerless, so we loved her all the more.

This went on for a few weeks until one Monday her mood changed. This morning as I walked up to the fence to feed her breakfast, Sunday opened her miniature donkey mouth wide, showed her buck teeth, and brayed uproariously, as if to say, "Hey! Where's my grain?"

Sunday was happy again, though I know she will always remember her child and continue to love her. The sheep were their normal persnickety selves, and the other animals were no longer hanging their heads.

Sunday is not alone in carrying that memory. I also carry it. It was a spiritual experience we shared that morning. The mother donkey and I were two beings coming together in a time of agonizing pain. I will never be the same. My love for animals, including their wisdom, their interconnection, and their love for each other is great, just as it is for humans.

Part Two

Theology

4
Seasons of Love
February 25, 2024

Do you sometimes do things out of your comfort zone for people you love, because you love them? Maybe you've been the momma bear who stood up for children and what they needed, even when it was uncomfortable? Or the neighbor who said yes when others looked away? Perhaps you've followed an urge to help someone or a group of people, even though it felt illogical or overwhelming.

Love has a way of doing that. It nudges us toward what we know is right and holy and good. It is up to us to decide to listen.

I have wanted to deliver this sermon about the meaning of Love for quite a while, but I resisted writing it because I didn't want to shortchange or do a disservice to Love's power and possibilities—until my resistance to sharing these ideas came right up against my commitment to someone I care about deeply. I chose Love.

Before I start, however, I need to say something to those of you who are doubting Love, or who have never felt or known its power. I have been there too. And, if it is helpful, I invite you to borrow my Love. Take as much as you need until you find your own.

My friend Polly was diagnosed with a serious illness a few months ago. Polly has been encouraging me to write this sermon for years. "I promise I will read it," she said. "I'll keep it on my nightstand and read it just before I go to sleep."

It was time to write this sermon. It was Love's season. I dedicate this sermon to Polly, to all of you, and to the mysterious, beautiful, bold, and subtle power called Love.

These reflections are solely my understanding of Love. You may or may not agree with what I'm saying. I'm not asking them to be yours and I'm not proselytizing. Each of us has our own understanding and experiences of Love. These are mine.

In her poem "I Feel Sorry for Jesus," Palestinian American poet Naomi Shihab Nye describes her frustration with people's blasphemous attributions to Jesus. Her feelings expressed in this poem illustrate how I feel about people's too frequent denigration of Love. Thus I share her poem as a way into my reflections on Love which will follow.

I Feel Sorry for Jesus

People won't leave Him alone.
I know He said, wherever two or more
are gathered in my name...
but I'll bet some days He regrets it.

Cozily they tell you what He wants
and doesn't want
as if they just got an e-mail.
Remember "Telephone," that pass-it-on game

where the message changed dramatically
by the time it rounded the circle?
Well.
People blame terrible pieties on Jesus.

They want to be his special pet.
Jesus deserves better.
I think He's been exhausted
for a very long time.

He went into the desert, friends.
He didn't go into the pomp.
He didn't go into
the golden chandeliers

and say, the truth tastes better here.
See? I'm talking like I know.
It's dangerous talking for Jesus.
You get carried away almost immediately.

I stood in the spot where He was born.
I closed my eyes where He died and didn't die.
Every twist of the Via Dolorosa
was written on my skin.

And that makes me feel like being silent
for Him, you know? A secret pouch

of listening. You won't hear me
mention this again.

I feel about Love the way the poet feels about Jesus. (Actually, I share her feelings about him too.)

Here are some of the things I hear about Love. *It doesn't work. Love is a cliché. Love is soft, meaningless. There are problems to be dealt with in the world. If Love is so powerful, why are there wars?*

I ask: Has Love really been tried? What kind of Love are you referring to? How do you define it?

Love saved my life.

Let me just start there. The Love I'm talking about wasn't given by a parent, grandparent, or romantic partner. Those people fell short in one way or another as all people do at some point. That kind of Love is a gift, but it isn't the only Love, and it's not the kind that will save us. We must touch into *that* Love ourselves.

Love as I understand and experience it is an energy, a power of good. We all have to make the decision to engage with it. This is always a choice, for unlike fear and violence, Love will not overpower you.

We all have equal access to Love's power, though many people have lost that connection because of a culture that doesn't value it, or by being mistreated by a person, people, or a system.

I know that disconnection; I have lived it, and I know it can be healed.

Allow me, if you will, to share my letter to my dear friend Polly, answering her question, What is Love?

Dear Polly, friend of mine, and many others,

Your smile is so bright, made more real by your deep dimples. Your optimism is present even while you know struggle, especially now that you know a different kind of pain.

Your light shines so bright it makes Hallmark look like CNN. I didn't believe it could be real at first.

So rare is this state of heart that you embody.

Over time I learned to believe it and trust that it is real.

Yet all the optimism and joy in the world does not make us immune from sickness, disease, and loss. (All the more reason to be joyful anyway!)

You've asked me for a long time, my friend, to write about my understanding of Love.

The day I saw your beautiful smile waver was the day I knew it was time to speak my truth aloud, for you.

Because that's what Love does.

Love enters into pain.

Love walks toward the places where too many people are afraid to go—the places where we feel the most alone and sometimes powerless.

Love holds space.

It holds memories if and until we are ready to remember.

Love is an ever-present energy we must choose, for fear, cynicism, and greed are always waiting by its side.

Love is relational. It is an exchange within ourselves, between two or more people or animals, and between people, animals, and the Earth. Love is experienced in the exchange between us and everything we value, including inanimate objects, musical instruments, or a favorite chair on the summer dock.

Love protects, even as it connects and ends isolation. It moves at our speed.

Love is beautiful, nowhere more poignant than when Love is felt in the hardest of times. Beautiful Love is when we cry and don't give a damn how we look. It is when we sob angry sobs, and our eyes are blood red. Beautiful Love is when we call and ask for help. Beautiful Love is when turn to another and say, "I see you" and mean it.

Love always moves toward the next right action. If we keep following it day by day it will lead us to the flowing river, the wellspring that bends toward unity, compassion, and truth.

Love is brave even as it is humble. It shows its strength in the places where intellect and heart intertwine. Brave Love is vulnerability, truth telling, and daring to take a risk.

At the same time, Love is paradoxical and mysterious. It is never changing and ever changing, personal and universal.

Love speaks all languages, even curse words and silence. Perhaps especially those.

Oh, and Love laughs, belly laughs and quiet laughs. Sometimes it laughs and cries at the same time.

Love has an uncanny ability to know where the need is and to go there.

Love is accessible regardless of physical distance because Love knows no boundaries; it is much larger than that.

Above all, dear One, as you sit where you are today, know that Love is eternal. It never ends with death. Love lives on and on and on, even in its changing form.

Love. Its circles are everywhere, through all the seasons of our life.

I love you, Polly.

What blocks us from choosing Love? Resentment, fear, loneliness, wounds from abuses of power that you inflicted or received. Does habit keep Love out or do we keep it out trying to be safe?

The other thing that can close us down to Love is loss. This is something less talked about but so important. There is nothing like the feelings we experience when we lose someone we love, whether through a long or sudden death. It can feel like a wasteland even as your refrigerator is overflowing with casseroles from friends.

When someone we care about is hurting, changing, growing old, or losing some abilities, the loss can be agonizing.

This agony generally stems from our guilt. *I shouldn't feel this way. We've been together so many years. He's my father or she's my mother.* With thoughts like these we cut ourselves off from self-compassion and grace. We expect ourselves to be grateful rather than grieving. Let's recognize that we can grieve the losses even as we also love this person more than words can say.

Change brings loss and loss brings grief. When we don't grieve well we have no choice but to suppress it or move away from anyone or anything that may touch that grief.

How many people are dying inside, longing for a friendly smile or hug, and yet too closed off to admit it? How many of us take these people at their word, or even worse, mistake their defenses for the truth?

We all love, my friends. We all love, and we all grieve. We all heal, and we all need Love. Forgiveness is one important part of this opening to Love. Forgiveness is not easy, and it is not either/or. Most of us forgive a little, but not everything. That's okay. Sometimes you wake up one day to realize there is nothing more to forgive, and sometimes you don't.

"Say 'I love you' before they die," says FRS member Ken Kretsch.

Love is a choice, sometimes easy and often hard.

Love goes to where it hurts and invites connection. However, all parties must choose Love in a relationship; it can't be one sided. In a group or country, enough people must choose to love so that it starts a groundswell of caring, holding, and repairing what is broken, hearts and all.

Choose well, my friends, with safe places and people. When it's unsafe to enter a space, relationship, or topic, stay away. Let others go into that pain with wisdom and boundaries them-selves. Move at your own pace and drop comparisons or feel-ings of despair.

Life is a series of seasons of hope, connection, and meaning. Seasons that come and go and come again. Birth, growth, death, rebirth.

Whether you are ready for a journey or caring for a loved one who once cared for you, they're all seasons. Each of these seasons has unique challenges and gifts.

Saints or ascended masters live in union with the energy of Love all the time. We are not saints. We are simply living our lives and doing our best. But trust this: Every action of Love you choose changes you and the recipient—if they are willing. Love just may change the world.

Start by picking one quality of Love. Move toward the pain, be brave, speak the truth, hold space for someone, and see how Love responds.

May ours be a place where Love grows.

May your seasons be seasons of Love.

5
To the Point
March 27, 2022

The reading referred to at the start of this sermon:

Moving Day
By Reverend Rebecca Bryan

We were moving and leaving that terrible house.
All my dreams were real.

My stepdad waits on the side of the driveway to embark.
He will drive ahead of us in his car.

I open the door to our blue car, put our poodle, Toby, in the
back seat, and strap him in. With my beloved mutt safe and
sound, I place my nine-year-old self in the front bucket seat,
next to my mom who will be driving.

She is sober.

Guided by Love

This makes my heart sing. My hopes rise, floating so high they
go magically out of the car roof, where they connect with the
white clouds high in the pale blue sky.

I follow them and catch a balloon floating by.

I return to my body and feel my hands on the vinyl car seat,
then turn to snap in the seat belt until I hear a pop,
so I know it's secure.
Safe, as I've always wanted to be.

Eventually I start to read. It feels like it's been an hour or two.
It may only have been five minutes.
Eternity knows no time in a child's life.
Vision remembers the worst; books promise the best.

Licking my pointer finger before turning the page, I reach my
hand down to the floor where our snacks are happily packed
in a bag. "Do you want a cheese cracker, mom?" I ask, as I
consider a prune for myself. The prunes must have been left
over when she emptied the cupboard.

I know the bright orange cheese crackers in their crinkly
plastic, six to a package, exactly six, were purchased just for
our trip. I pretend not to notice or care that they are store
brands, not real. Generic stands in for most anything in our
home. For those years of my life we knew Green Stamps,
rotten stale food on sale, and generic.
For the first time it doesn't matter.
My happiness no longer depends on her.

To the Point

We follow my stepfather's car safely, keeping two car lengths
between us.

And then she does it—pulls the Budweiser out from behind
her seat and opens it with one hand. That awful popping
sound rings danger in my ear as she drives with her free hand.
Swinging the beer to her mouth, she chugs it and then pats
my leg. "It's going to be different this time," she says.
"I promise."

FRS parishioner Nancy Crochiere asked me if I would prefer
to read the piece you just heard, since I wrote it. I told her it
would be preferable, by far, if she read it, because I have
learned that pain is not meant to be held alone and that it
certainly can't be healed alone, at least not in my experience.

And that's what I'm offering you this morning—my experience.
It may or may not have similarities to your life experiences,
and I'm not trying to persuade you to believe anything. This is
my way of letting you get to know me better, specifically from
the perspective of my faith journey and interior life. I hope we
can all find ways to share our truths with one another, be it in
word, art, or intimate conversations. If not here at church, then
where?

I am moved to share with you my Journey of Faith for several
reasons. First, I have been impressed by the Journeys of Faith
I've heard here in the last four years and by the testimonials
shared over this past month. Every time one of you tells your
story, I am made better. Your truths enrich my experience and
understanding of life. Your stories make me laugh, cry, ques-

tion, and wonder. That, then, is my hope: that each of you may laugh, cry, question, wonder, or in some way be changed by what you hear this morning.

I am also sharing this morning because I cringe whenever I hear someone question whether this church has spirituality at its center, along with caring for one another and working for social justice. "Do they know me?" I ask myself when I hear that question. It would be impossible for me to be a minster without being spiritual. It is foundational to who I am. My spirituality and faith are the sources of my strength, energy, and inspiration. It is essential to who I am: It's time for me to be perfectly clear about this aspect of myself.

Lastly, I am sharing today because I want to model authentic connection. I hope my words and truth help even one person. I am no longer willing to hide.

Before I go on, let me set down on the proverbial table a few facts, that are not easy facts. You've heard many of them over the last four years although I've never put them all together nor been quite as specific as I will be now.

I am a survivor of child abuse that went on for years, including sexual abuse at tender young ages. Those experiences made lasting impressions and deep wounds on my heart, my psyche, and my mind. But they do not define me. They do not have the final word. I survived. I heal and thrive, every day, after years of transformative and sometimes grueling work.

The abuse and alcoholism rampant in my mother's home, where these things occurred, caused many painful patterns I have had to overcome, including addiction, PTSD, and faulty thinking about myself and the world around me. I turned to food as a source of medication and dissociation when this all started when I was four years old.

Later in life, and for a much shorter stint, I turned to alcohol. Not surprisingly, I was a magnet to sick men, particularly those in power, such as bosses and professors, resulting in further mistreatment and abuse.

Through it all, what saved me was my faith that things would get better someday. And they have, beyond my wildest dreams. For that I am grateful. I will always turn around and look for those who I can help know freedom. I have deep gratitude for the many people who have loved me and supported me, some of whom are watching this online, my father who always believed in me, and always my beloved children and husband.

The framework within which I experience and express my spirituality is multifaceted. I was born a mystic and religious naturalist; I just came out that way. This means that I experience the God of my understanding daily, sometimes in small ways, sometimes miraculously, and always in nature, as well as in relationship.

My sensitivity to and awareness of the unitive experience of life started young. In my earliest memory of seeing a spirit, I saw an Indigenous person on the land where I was living. I was three years old. This shamanistic experience of life—the connection to the nonphysical and intuitive realms—is second nature to me. It is an important way that I see the world.

My parents separated when I was four, after which time I was raised by my mother in the Methodist church. I loved church, as I've mentioned before from this pulpit. I loved its red carpets, safe feelings, and people all around. We rarely went to worship services though, so I was never indoctrinated in religious teachings. Most of what I knew about spirituality and God came from within me.

I converted to Unitarian Universalism at the age of nine when I first heard a UU minister preach at my grandparents' church in Brewster, Massachusetts. "This just makes sense," I thought. I later converted to Catholicism for seven years while married to my first husband, so we would share a faith in which to raise our children.

But I never left any of my earlier threads. I wove them into the person I was becoming—shaman, mystic, religious naturalist, Christian, and Unitarian Universalist.

I started practicing yoga in my twenties. It has been a continuing and essential way I have learned to be in my body, and it connects body and spirit. It continues to be a daily practice for me, though its forms and lineage have changed over time.

As a young adult, I also began learning and integrating into my life Buddhist practices including meditation and mindfulness. Pema Chödrön and Thich Nhat Hanh continue to be key teachers in my pluralistic knapsack.

Twelve-step recovery programs have been essential to my life for the past fifteen years and are foundational to how I live my life. For me, these programs are both spiritual and humanist, with sustaining approaches to life that I was never taught as a child.

One year after I stopped drinking, I started seminary, which had been calling me for decades. Soon I realized how important it was for me to be clean if I was to grow into my true self. My time in seminary was a dream come true in all ways and led me to ordination in 2015 and to you in 2018.

The older I get the more connected I am to feminism, womanist theology, and to writing as a spiritual, healing, and creative practice. I am attracted to bold women who walk their true path, like Dorothy Day, Jaqui Lewis, and Nadia Weber Boltz, and to other more reserved women like Julian of Norwich and Sue Monk Kidd.

In my faith journey, there are three through lines which have remained through all its twists and turns. These golden threads weave in and out of my everyday life experience.

God is real.

Healing and transformation are possible with authentic love and connection.

There is more to reality than meets the human eye.

God is real. By God, I mean a force of nature always available to us. It is a good thing. It is our choice to connect with this energy, yet it will always be there to help us connect with our best selves and whatever it is that we need at that moment, be it patience, courage, wisdom, compassion, and even rage. I call it Love.

Mine is a theology of a real and loving source which I call God, which embraces all, and with which we can freely choose to be in relation.

In this understanding, God is more of an energy than a person. It is at the same time personal and impersonal, expansive, and microcosmic. God does not control but offers itself. Therefore, as I understand it

God is chosen

God is love

God is brave, forgiving, and compassionate

God is fierce, strong, and beautiful

God knows no gender and

God moves toward justice, compassion, and communal liberation

This evergreening source, or love, is always available to everyone.

It is experienced through authentic connection within ourselves, between two or more people, and with the source itself. It is expressed through courageous action that works for the liberation and equality of all people, the Earth, and its creatures.

I communion, or come into contact and relationship with this source, in silence *and* in action. I need both for my theology to be grounded and authentic at this point in my life. I am healthiest when I have a rich inner life and outer life. I wake up before sunrise at 4 a.m. every day to relish two hours of uninterrupted spiritual practice. It is my soul's food.

My work in justice must, by necessity, be balanced with contem-plative practices of centering prayer, silence, being with nature, writing, and connecting to my inner world. The silence calls me to engage in compassionate, brave action for all who suffer, and my work in the world demands that I return to silence and connec-tion, where I replenish and restore both my body and my soul.

I am a devoted follower of the life and teachings of Jesus, including giving priority to the marginalized, speaking truth to power, practicing nonviolence and inclusion, and demon-strating radical, radical love. I avoid intellectual debate about Jesus but find his teachings and way of life compelling and interesting.

I am a Unitarian Universalist minister who believes in the necessity and beauty of religious plurality and the right of all people to their beliefs. I am a pacifist and spiritual warrior who does her best to live by the values of love, courage, and beauty. I seek to be rigorously honest with myself and radi-cally compassionate with others.

I believe in and find much guidance and nurturance from the spiritual realm including guides, spirits, and the unseen. There is more than meets the human eye.

Above all, my faith is one of hope—hope that things will get better and that healing and transformation are possible. I know this is possible on a personal level, as I've lived it in my own life and supported many others in their own transforma-tion. Because I believe that what is true on the micro level is also true on the macro level, I believe healing and transforma-tion are possible on the public level. If, in my experience, we choose God, or love, we connect in authentic relationship, act with courage, and realize there is always more than meets the eye.

6
Unfolding
December 8, 2019

"God is not inevitable."

I was sitting in meditation when this thought came to me. "God is not inevitable." It brought me great joy. I felt like a light had been turned on in my mind, leaving years of spiritual seeking, questioning, and learning hanging in abeyance.

I had been living with a spiritual conundrum for decades. I felt as though, and sometimes even *knew* intuitively that, there is more to life than meets the eye. I longed for a connection to that something greater, larger than I, a guiding force of love. I grew up steeped in Western thought, philosophy, and religion, specifically Christianity. God was portrayed as male, a being not of this realm that never changed. Above all, God was all-powerful. As you might imagine, the contrast between what I experienced and what I was taught caused conflict within me.

How could this all-powerful God *cause* bad things to happen in this world? Worse yet, how could God possibly *allow evil to exist?*

Why weren't my prayers answered? I knew the anthropomorphized white, male, bearded God in the sky wasn't real, and yet my longing for God, whatever that was, never stopped. It was maddening, distressing, and sometimes all-consuming.

My efforts to reconcile all of this included trying to not believe in anything spiritual, returning to the beliefs of my childhood, and exploring many different religions. The one thing that didn't occur to me was that my underlying assumptions were wrong, assumptions like God is all-powerful, all-knowing, and never-changing. I kept trying to solve my quandary by either changing the extrapolations of these underlying premises or discarding the premises entirely. The one philosophy that allows me to integrate my rational mind and spiritual longings is *process theology.*

I was introduced to process theology during seminary. It intrigued me then, but it didn't change me. My recent revelation during meditation, that "God is not inevitable," led me to revisit and reconsider what process theology has to offer. It has been a joyous, an exciting, and most of all a liberating experience.

Process theology, or process philosophy as it was originally termed, was developed by Alfred North Whitehead in the 1920s. Whitehead was a British mathematician and philosopher looking for a unifying, underlying theory that could apply to and explain everything. His resultant process theology has been furthered by various academics, philosophers, and theologians. The Reverend Dr. Martin Luther King, Jr. wrote his dissertation on a process theologian named Henry Nelson

Wieman. The principles of this thinking have striking resonance with our Unitarian Universalist principles.

Sources of information for this sermon come from the writings of Alfred Whitehead as analyzed by one of his mentees, Robert Mesle, and from two contemporary sources: Adrienne Maree Brown, an activist and student of Octavia Brown and Grace Lee Boggs, and Rabbi Bradley Shavit Artson, the first Jewish theologian and non-Christian to apply this philosophy to their religion. I have particularly enjoyed and learned a lot from Rabbi Artson's book, *God of Becoming and Relationship*. If anyone is interested in reading and discussing it, please let me know. I'd be happy to facilitate a discussion group.

Process theology can be summarized by this sentence: *We live in and are co-creators of a connected, relational, dynamic universe*. This means that the future is not predetermined. Though the past is an indelible part of that yet-to-be-determined future, we still have choices. Thus, how we act matters. If we are part of this connected, relational, dynamic universe, then so is everyone and everything else, including all people, the Earth and her creatures, and God.

Process theologians believe God is not an ever-constant, all-knowing force outside of this universe. Rather, they believe that God is a part of the universe, malleable and changed as a result of the decisions being made every day by humans and other living creatures. Yes, process theologians believe that God changes. Artson writes:

> The world and God are expressions of continuous, dynamic relational change. We and the world are not solid substances, but rather recurrent patterns of

43

energy, occasions that change with each new instantiation, but also maintain continuity from moment to moment. We are interconnected, each to each and each to all. Therefore, all creation–not just humanity or a subset of humanity–has value and dignity. We respond to the decisions of each other and of the totality, as we ourselves are re-created in each instant.[13]

For those of you who enjoy quantum physics, this may sound familiar. For example, consider Brownian Motion or Random Walk, which our congregant Ken Kretsch taught me about in our most recent conversation. Brownian Motion is how molecules relate to one another in air. The molecules run parallel to each other until they collide, at which point each molecule veers off in a new direction, changed by the interaction. You can't predict where things will go. Every collision is the result of many collisions in the past, each leading toward the present moment. This is known as a Random Walk.

It's important to discuss how process thinkers understand and define God. For them, God is a source of goodness, ever-present, but not all-powerful or all-knowing. Therefore, predestination does not exist. God understands the past and invites us to choose our actions. God is an energy that actually makes our relating possible. God does not coerce. God persuades.

Mesle writes, "...In the fullest sense possible, then, God is love: God is perfect relational power."[14] He goes on to describe God in terms of relatedness and process rather than an unchanging, static being unaffected by the world.[15]

This way of thinking allows us to consider God anew. Artson writes that people in the West assume the only way to understand religion is by applying traditional Western thought including dualism, which forces us to choose between mind and body, science and faith, spiritual and physical. "They take neo-Platonized Aristotelian scholastic presuppositions and filter religion through those ideas."[16]

Mesle writes about the possibilities that come with applying the process thinking of connected relationality over dualistic Platonic thinking: "...we could finally leave behind the last vestiges of Cartesian dualism...and...see ourselves as 100 percent natural instances of the larger world around us."[17]

What does all of this mean? What are the possible implications as they relate to joy and our day-to-day lives? I answer those questions with two words: wonder and responsibility. Thinking from a process approach allows us to experience wonder, amazement, and joy and to be touched by the world. At the same time, it creates a sense of responsibility, calling us to respond to what we experience in this world in ways that point toward good, wholeness, and equity for all living beings.

Living in a dualistic world, believing we must choose between our head and our heart, between spirituality and reason, and science and faith, leads us to be cut off from our own integrated self and thus from the interconnected web of which we are a part.

Whitehead believed that "morality is tied up with the breadth of vision..." and said, "If I see my life as totally disconnected from others, no moral vision is possible."[18]

As co-creators living with the knowledge that we are connected to all, there is no other option but to act in ways that uphold and further the inherent worth and dignity of all people.

A colleague of mine uses process theology to talk to the youth in her congregation about God. In youth group one day, she was asked if she believed in God. She answered "Yes" and then explained what that means to her. "Think of the Boston Marathon bombing," she told them, "...and remember the people who ran back into the explosion and flames, risking their safety to rescue other people. That is God, as I understand God." I agree.

These people at the bombing were faced with a decision. They certainly didn't ask to be in the situation they found themselves in that day: victims of a bombing. It was, as we discussed earlier, an example of Brownian Motion or Random Walk of life. They chose to follow the persuasion that called them toward love. We are faced with decisions hundreds of times each day, most apparently innocuous, but are they?

Fred Rogers, may he rest in peace, told children to look for the helpers in any crisis. Yes, and as adults we are also called to be those helpers so that when our children look for them, helpers exist.

We can choose to lean into what is unfolding, act in love, and allow that same love to support us. It isn't about whether our actions are big or small. We generally don't know the results of our actions. Choosing love includes writing a postcard to Unitarian Universalists who are incarcerated, to let them know they are not forgotten, visiting homebound congregants and delivering the beautiful ornaments our children are making right now in Young Church, getting proximate to people who are oppressed, or sending loving kindness in your meditations.

Contrary to what the media may want us to believe, it is in our DNA to do this, to follow the persuasion of goodness. Rebecca Solnit studies how people react in times of crisis. Her book, *A Paradise Built in Hell*, tells stories of crises, including the 1906 San Francisco earthquake, 9-11, and Hurricane Katrina. In all of these situations and more, most people reacted with selflessness, benevolence, and love toward their fellows. People grew closer during the crises, building community through their shared challenges.

Solnit writes, "When all the ordinary divides and patterns are shattered, people step up—not all, but the great preponderance—to become their brothers' keepers. And that purposefulness and connectedness bring joy even amid death, chaos, fear and loss."[19]

Whether or not process theology appeals to you, Unitarian Universalists believe that revelation is not sealed. We are part of what is called a living tradition. We believe in dialectical humanism. This means that we will change as a result of learning new information and will come to believe something different from what we had believed before. This is at the core of process thinking and process theology.

At every moment we can decide whether to choose love, or God, to use the terms of process theologians. In other words, God is not inevitable. It is our choice whether to choose God.

Above all, process thinking asks us to open ourselves and to see what is unfolding within, around, and between us. In her poem "The Servant-Girl at Emmaus," Denise Levertov reminds us of this need to see—referring to the people that do not recognize the risen deity:

> Those who had brought this stranger home to
>   their table
> don't recognize yet with whom they sit.
> But she in the kitchen, absently touching
> the wine jug she's to take in,
> a young Black servant intently listening,
>
> swings round and sees
> the light around him
> and is sure.[20]

At that moment, the Brownian Movement or Random Walk, when the past comes together and two things connect in the present, the servant has a choice to see. I have no doubt how she will respond.

Part Three

Humanism

7
The Myths and Gifts of Normalcy

August 27, 2023

This sermon was delivered at the First Congregational Society Unitarian Church of Hampton Falls, New Hampshire. The church is a one-room chapel in the middle of a New Hampshire field, adjacent to an apple orchard. First Religious Society ministers have preached a service there each summer for decades.

I love being here to preach each August. It is beautiful inside, with its trompe l'oeil paintings and reed organ. It is beautiful outside, with the waving meadows, farmland, and trees. Over the years, we have gathered here on cloudy days, on rainy days, and on bright sunny mornings like today.

It is a tradition, or one might say, an old-fashioned way that this congregation and my congregation in Newburyport have joined for decades. The ministers of the First Religious Society come here rain or shine, in all ages and stages of their ministries.

I love preparing and delivering these late August sermons because they don't need to communicate a vital message of where the congregation is in its journey, nor make an appeal for money, nor solve the justice issue of the day. They can just be normal. They can meander, wander, wonder, and pause to consider daily living. They are exquisite in this normalcy. Being average certainly doesn't mean that they are unnecessary sermons. What is our attachment to greatness anyway?

When did the pursuit of greatness become more important than knowing our exquisiteness?

Greatness is overrated in our society, at least in the middle- and upper-middle-class, largely white neighborhoods along the Eastern Seaboard of the United States. Children are taught to pursue greatness, to be the best at whatever endeavor they try. This relentless pursuit of greatness has changed people's perceptions so that being average tends to be seen as being a failure. What is average, then? How can everyone be great?

The truth is that we are not necessarily great, certainly not in everything we do, nor throughout our lives. Most of us are more or less average. *And at the same time, our mere existence is exquisite.*

The myth of greatness applies equally to adults as to children, including adults in the last decades of their lives. All too many of these older adults worry that their lives were not lived well enough. In their final years they are concerned that they made mistakes or mis-prioritized. "What is my legacy?" people often ask me at the end of their lives.

It's a fallacy that legacy is only for the great and the high achievers. Your life is your legacy. Your ordinary, exquisite self is your legacy. That is true for those who are great and who have achieved as well.

We don't miss greatness when people die. We miss their ordinariness. We miss their lumpy mashed potatoes and their tendencies to always think they know the answers. We miss their vulnerabilities and their smiles with wrinkles on their beloved faces.

On reading the title of this sermon, FRS member Wendy Ford sent me an email sharing how important the concept of normalcy is to her and her adult children.

With her permission, I share her words:

> The very word (normalcy) has held special meaning for me ever since my fabulous husband, who had to go all too soon, said—just after we received the devastating diagnosis—that it was all that he wanted (normalcy). I suppose I am always trying to keep his spirit alive—or at least available. He was extraordinary, and his wish for Normalcy truly did set the children and me down such a healthy path.

> "You probably have your sermon for this Sunday all set, but I couldn't help noticing the subject. I believe that my book, Normalcy, is still on the FRS site, and I just wanted you to know that you are welcome to any part of it that you might find helpful.

Thank you, Wendy.

When my own father died a few months ago, I wanted two things of his: anything that had his handwriting on it and one of his flannel shirts. I didn't care about his big accomplishments, diplomas from prestigious schools, or work awards. I wanted to feel him, see his handwriting, and remember his everyday normal self.

In addition to blinding us to the exquisiteness of life, the pursuit of greatness feeds the myth that we are alone and somehow flawed, while everyone else has it all together. I can assure you this is not true, nor should it be.

I learned a long time ago that there is nothing any of us experience, feel, question, or believe that others don't also experience, feel, question, and believe. We must be brave enough to talk about what we are experiencing and feeling, appropriately, and have community and friends who are willing to share their experiences seriously too. Consider the myths of seeking and experiencing perpetual good health or having a particular sized or abled body if you eat the right foods. These are untrue and dangerous myths that drive us to turn against our own bodies. It is human to be imperfect, flawed, average, and aging. It is human to be normal and it is human to be exquisite at the same time. Both are part of being normal. These are liberating truths.

Here, on this exquisite Sunday, we get to be normal together. We get to rejoice in what is good, beautiful, and true.

Let's celebrate the ordinary: flannel shirts, jean jackets, dogs, and fireflies.

Let's celebrate children's sticky hands that leave a mess on the windowpanes and kitchen cupboards.

Let's celebrate our aching bodies and our aching backs, which make reaching and tying our shoes more difficult.

Let's celebrate what we *can* do and the exquisite world of which we are part—its beauty, fragility, and the care we must give it.

I believe Life created every part of creation, including you, to be exquisite just as you are. I don't believe Life cares about greatness. I do believe it celebrates our gifts and our efforts.

May we all remember the gifts of normalcy. May we make room to do things that are time-consuming, even old-fashioned, that are unnecessary, and that are, most definitely, kind.

8
Dreams
August 21, 2022

When you're young, time seems eternal, doesn't it?

Do you remember being in high school or perhaps college, or remember being a young parent? Do you remember when dreams were all you knew to think about, and nothing seemed impossible?

Or perhaps you were told not to dream too big and buried what your heart called you to do in this world. Or at least you tried to bury it.

How do we befriend what life has brought us? How do we make peace with the decisions made for us, as well as those we made ourselves?

When I was the ripe age of 24, a nun told me that I was naïve and that someday I would realize what was reasonable and what was fanciful. I was working in a Youth Service Bureau with parents, many of them involved with the Department of Child Protective Services. I wanted to save the world, especially children, and ensure that they were seen. I'm sure my work did matter and helped some families, and some of the children live on in my heart to this day.

But child abuse continues. I did not save the world.

It was not for nothing, though, that I gave all that I had to that work. Caring means something, and outcomes are not the only measure of success.

Our dreams matter, whether they are or are not realized exactly as we imagine they will be. Our dreams tell us much about who we are and what matters to us.

Naivety can be beautiful and may be a necessity for hope to live on in this world. Someone must act as the ploughshare and believe this time can be different.

I've learned and am learning not to regret any of my dreams, but to honor and learn from them all, including those that went awry, those that happened differently from what I had hoped, and those that never happened at all.

What does it take to realize such a relationship with ourselves? First and foremost, it takes self-compassion. Do you believe that you have done the best you could do in this lifetime? Do you recognize that everyone makes mistakes and most of us make big mistakes?

What if our dreams are not to be measured, but treasured? What if they are a map of our soul?

Time is not eternal, my friends. Well, time may be, but our time on Earth is not. We will all come to the end of our days but can hope to arrive there with a combination of dreams realized and dreams still to be realized. I invite you all to befriend your dreams, to ask yourselves what your dreams are telling you about who you are and what matters most to you. Then ask yourself if there are other ways to manifest what matters. Join your dreams as partners. They are some of the most important companions we can have.

9

When More Is Not Enough

November 21, 2021

A sermon delivered on Zoom for a
Thanksgiving service during COVID-19

How do we know when enough is enough?

How can we tell if our appetite is satisfied or even sated?

I don't know about you, but my sense of satisfaction, or "enoughness," was broken long ago. For much of my life, I repeatedly passed the state of enough and moved to being sated, or beyond full, be it with food, responsibilities, or even self-improvement. It seemed that no matter how much I tried, it was never enough. And I still struggle with knowing I'm enough, though it's getting better all the time.

"Enough is as good as a feast" is one of my favorite quotations, introduced to me by parishioner Merryl Maleska Wilbur. I find the old English saying provocative; it makes me stop and think. Its pithiness demonstrates its truth: "Enough is as good as a feast."

I acknowledge that I have written this morning's reflection for those who have the privilege and burden of being able to overconsume. Many in life are not so privileged. I recognize that.

For those who can overconsume—and I can only speak from that place in life—the question, "*When is enough, enough?*" is challenging and, I believe, critical.

When does *more* become not *enough*, but destructive? In the simplest of terms, we know we've had enough when we are able to appreciate what we are consuming and what we are doing or experiencing and appreciate the company of our companions if we are not alone. Eating enough food leaves our bellies feeling secure and contained. We smile and maybe even salivate when we remember what we just ate. Enjoying enough company with others brings us a sense of belonging, connection, or stimulation. We finish the exchange differently from where we started, having met our social or intellectual needs. Engaging in *enough* web surfing gives us the information we need to write a paper or make an informed decision. We may finish the research more curious, assured, or confused; regardless, we remember what it was we were researching when we started.

On the other hand, more than enough food leaves us feeling physically uncomfortable, often regretful, and sometimes even ashamed. "How did I do it again? It was only going to be one piece of pie." When we've had more than enough company, we might stop listening, start to check out, or become insensitive in our interactions. When we have exceeded a healthy amount of screen time, we can be disorientated, discon-nected, and drained.

I find that living in accordance with the principle of *enough* allows me to experience genuine gratitude, connection, and even bliss. Those feelings don't happen when I overindulge in anything.

Lest I make this sound easy, I assure you it is not, at least in my experience. For most of us, this process of consuming enough, whether it is physical, mental, or social, is something we learn to do, unless we are so fortunate as to have been taught otherwise. Maybe we were parented perfectly and lived unaffected by the prevailing culture around us, a culture that promotes more than enough through marketing, portion sizes, and addictive technology.

The value of moderation, or "enoughness," is an ancient truth. Two of the three inscriptions on a column before the Temple of Delphi read: *Know thyself* and *Nothing in excess*. (The third was *Surety brings ruin.)*

Why then is enoughness so difficult to carry out? There are many answers to that. I'll offer one example on each of the physical, mental, and spiritual levels. Physically, it is chal-lenging for many of us to stay in our bodies. We have learned to dissociate, distract, or intellectualize every time we get too close to a feeling, especially if it's challenging. Mentally, we have bought into a lie that more is better. Sadly, this lie can also carry into our spirituality.

William Blake knew this when he wrote:

To see a World in a Grain of Sand,
And a Heaven in a Wild Flower,
Hold Infinity in the palm of your hand,
And Eternity in an hour.[21]

Can you remember when you experienced eternity in a moment? Maybe it was as recent as this morning; perhaps it was long ago. The *Encyclopedia Britannica* was my entry into eternity that years later the World Wide Web stole from me.

Picture if you will some 45 years ago, when I was ten years old. I raised my hand in history class and asked a question I don't even remember. The teacher's response was predictable: "I don't know...Why don't you find out?" I needed the exact words that would gain me a hall pass to go to the library where answers lay hidden on the bookshelves. My saddle shoes made a certain clumpy sound as I skipped across the linoleum floors to the library. I pulled up a stool to the stacks, stood on my tippy toes, and held my breath in anticipation. The heavy volume nearly dropped into my loving embrace, and I carried it to the long wooden table and opened it with a gasp. The pictures, the words, the worlds— eternity—and sooner or later, an answer to the question I had asked, whatever that was.

I still remember the sense of devastation I felt fifteen years later when the World Wide Web came on the scene. Somehow, I knew it ran the risk of robbing me of the chance to meet eternity in my quest for truth, the eternity I found when I put my hands on the pages of books, whose scent, words, and images opened up the world. *More was not better.*

True to the inkling, I must be careful about how quickly and frequently I turn to look online for answers and for what duration. The information I find there is often suspect in source, distracting if not overwhelming, and lacking any invitation to eternity.

How then do we master this skill of taking in enough?

First, it is critical to remember that what is enough differs for you and me. I cannot consume sugar, I need to sharply limit television input, and I find more than one party on any day to be too much. On the other hand, the two hours of spiritual practice I spend in meditation and prayer each morning would be intolerable for anyone else in my family.

Second, consuming enough needs to be something we consciously and consistently choose. It starts with our mind. In her book *Rising Strong*, sociologist and author Brené Brown says: "For me, the opposite of scarcity is not abundance. It's enough. I'm enough. My kids are enough."[22]

My wish for you this Thanksgiving is that you take the time to experience *enough*, whether it is looking at one flower, taking a long walk with nothing else to do, or having a single conversation with a neighbor or the family member who gets under your skin.

May you experience the miracle of eternity that comes with enough and nothing more.

10

Peace in the Day-to-Day

Christmas Eve 2022

When people's lives change—for instance, when children go off to school for the first time or when a loved one dies— it is everyday interactions that are missed the most.

We miss the banging of the screen door as our loved ones enter or leave the house. We long to hear the sound of the kettle boiling as we did each morning when our loved one brewed their tea. We would do anything to wipe off the sticky handprints left from their cooking.

Yes, it is the day-to-day that we miss when loved ones' lives change and we no longer live together. We miss the ordinari-ness of living that brings us the rhythms of our day-to-day routines. We realize how much we loved the person's predictable behaviors, endearing and irritating alike. We realize we even miss the person telling the same story again and again, which used to drive us crazy. *It is in the ordinari-ness of lives that peace exists.*

I believe that as Mary rocked her newborn Christ child, it wasn't magical, although it often gets portrayed that way. Jesus' birth was very ordinary: a babe in arms, stable animals around, animals appearing as friends.

Wise people knew Jesus' birth was sacred and offered gifts, saying "Remember these times. Mark these days. For they are filled with gifts that will sustain you, this day and in the days to come." Our elders often remind us of these same truths today.

Ordinary days and their memories help to form our lives. When we recognize the sacredness of the ordinary we can choose to:

Fold the sweater as we take it from the dryer with care.

Answer the phone call from our relative with love and presence.

Open our eyes each morning and say, "Thank you."

Walk through our days in astonished gratitude.

Take note as you perform these daily actions. Emblazon the memories of these actions and the accompanying feelings on your heart, so that you can call on them in the future, time and again. In so doing the memories will always be there when you need them. The feeling of peace will return in the form of a story or memory you have revisited hundreds of times.

Love and peace never die; they are with us always. The peace of the ordinary will always come through when we're open to it. So may it be this day and every day throughout the year to come.

11
Suffering Explored
April 19, 2020

"Go ahead. Let it out, honey. I am not afraid of your pain."

It had been six months since my last drink. Twenty-five Friday evenings without any red wine. My emotions were as present as I had ever felt them. It felt like I was going to crawl out of my skin.

I called a dear friend out of desperation. I was not so accustomed to asking for help at that point in my life. But I could not carry this pain alone. It needed to be held, witnessed— loved, if you will. Without such care, I would surely drink again or find some other means of anesthetizing myself.

My friend responded to me with exactly what I needed: unconditional love, unwavering presence, and no judgment. I could feel it over the telephone line, especially when she said, "I am not afraid of your pain." No one had ever said that to me before.

That experience changed me. I had been loved, witnessed, and held just as I was. My friend did not attempt to fix, pity, or deny my pain.

"You may forget with whom you laughed, but you will never forget with whom you wept,"[23] wrote Khalil Gibran.

"I am not afraid of your pain."

I have said those same words many times over the ensuing years...

> ...to the transgender woman, near her death, who wanted to know if she was forgiven. "I am not afraid of your pain."
>
> ...to the couple who asked if I would bless their babies before they were born, knowing they were likely to die during birth. "I am not afraid of your pain."
>
> ...to a family anguished over the change in their teenage son's behavior and his near fatal overdose. "I am not afraid of your pain."

"Isn't it depressing, spending so much time working with people during their difficulties in life?" my daughter once asked me.

"No," I answered. "I call it being with people in the underside of the belly. It's a place I'm quite comfortable with. I've met angels in human skin there, people who are unguarded, open, and real. They've taught me a lot including what you might fear when you are sick, what you often think about before you die, and what matters most in life. They are some of my biggest teachers, and for that I am immensely grateful."

I've learned that we are not all comfortable with suffering. I've come to understand that not everyone identifies with suffering or shares my love of being in the underside of the belly. I've heard a lot about suffering from people:

Suffering is something *other* people experience.

The concept of suffering reminds me of Christian teachings in which we are to "suffer for our sins."

Whenever I got sad, my parents told me to "Think of the starving children in Africa," who had it so much worse than I did.

I wonder sometimes if it is "un-American" to identify with suffering. Many of us were taught that it is selfish to think we suffer when we are so privileged or taught that the goal in life is to not suffer. It seems like we may be comfortable talking about emotional pain, loss, or grief, but not suffering.

Is suffering the same as pain?

"I haven't touched a human being in so long," someone said on the news the other night, referring to the experience of self-quarantine. Is that suffering?

The question I hear most frequently on this topic of suffering is "*Can I be joyful in the face of suffering? Is it wrong to be happy when there is so much suffering in the world?*"

Perhaps it is best at this point for me to define what I mean by suffering. Suffering, as I'm using it today, is part of the human condition. The Merriam-Webster dictionary defines suffering as "to feel or endure pain, illness, or injury."

You could replace the word suffering with grief, insecurity, or loss. It is a feeling or state of being wherein we are not free, emotionally, spiritually, and sometimes physically. When we suffer, we know there are things happening beyond our control, even as we recognize what we can control. When we love, we risk suffering. The Buddha taught that you will not find a person's life that, at some point, doesn't include suffering.

Understanding suffering and knowing how to relate to it is important, whether you have suffered in the past, are currently suffering, love someone who is suffering, or all three. We will all witness and experience suffering or pain at some point in our lives. Most of us will experience it many times.

World religions deal with suffering differently. Buddhism understands enlightenment as the end of suffering, with bodhisattvas being people who return to Earth time and again until all people are free from suffering. Hinduism teaches that we reincarnate as many times as necessary until we have sufficient grace to dissolve into energy that is God. Christianity has a range of responses to suffering, from understanding it as punishment for our sins, to seeing it as a call for utmost faith in the will of God.

As a liberal religion, we have less trouble understanding why suffering happens. William Murray, in his book *A Faith for All Seasons*, writes that Unitarian Universalists understand suffering to be a combination of the results of human freedom, the inhumanity of people toward one another, and the interconnectedness of the universe and randomness.[24]

Understanding the why of things, however, does not teach us how to live with suffering. How do we learn not to fear pain, our own and others? And why does it matter?[25]

It matters because living into our Unitarian Universalist principles and our Affirmation of Faith calls us to do so. "Love is the doctrine of this church. Service is its prayer." We say those words each week, as people have been doing in our sanctuary for thirty-nine years. To love is to encounter suffering as well as joy. To serve is to encounter suffering as well as to help find meaning in life.

Our principles articulate our promises to employ reason with faith, to honor and protect the interdependent web of life, and to work for justice and compassion in all human relations. Reason and science tell us there is suffering. The world needs us to be compassionate, caring, engaged people who can feel its pain. That world may be your family, our church community, or the wider world.

In my life I've learned to be comfortable with pain largely by using Buddhist and humanist practices. I think of it as a circle.

At the top of the circle is an **experience of suffering**. You lose your job. You don't know when you will see your grandchildren again. The first stop on the circular journey is to remember that this suffering will end. Everything changes. This too shall change.

Next, I need to **remember that I am not unique or alone**. At the very moment I am suffering, there are millions of other people suffering, many for the same reasons I am suffering.

The third stop on the circle is to **stay**. Feel my feelings so I do not numb out to all of life or become stuck in this suffering. Stay in my body. Stay with the experience. Stay connected to myself and others. Stay—it's that simple and that difficult. Many of us are not taught how to stay. We are taught to run, fight, deny.

Rounding the top of the circle I **realize that it will happen again**. Pain will happen. It may be the cycle of the same issue at a deeper level or a new issue. But suffering will come again, not because I'm doing anything wrong, but because it is part of life.

And when it does come, I will remember that it will pass. I am not alone. And perhaps most importantly, I am more than my suffering.

When I do those things, I can surrender to what is. Suffering loses its power over me. I can better choose how to respond to what is happening. Catastrophic thinking has less space. I can become curious, look for learning opportunities, and feel the preciousness of life.

This is the deep dive and the dance that I think we need to be brave enough to have out loud—naming and sharing suffering so that we all become stronger, more compassionate, and more open to what life offers.

I answer "yes" to the question "Do we have the right to be joyful in the face of suffering?" We must experience joy to give us the staying power and perspective that suffering requires. As deeply as it hurts is as deeply as we are called to love and choose a life of meaning.

We are more than our suffering. My prayer is that you always remember that. We are so much more than our suffering.

12
In the Companionship of Grief
February 5, 2023

I had avoided the office for some time, choosing to work in the meditation room instead of in my home office, from which I had led the congregation through COVID.

I knew I was avoiding my office, but I ignored the niggling sense that something was incomplete. "I just want a change of pace," I said to myself. Little did I know that it was grief I was avoiding. In avoiding my home office, I was eluding the loss that was held there.

For eighteen months, plus another two months later, I ministered to you over a screen. We held staff meetings, an annual congregational meeting, board meetings, and more—all online and all with me in my home office. The church building was closed except on the Sundays when I came to preach; at those services only our Director of Church Music, AV coordinator, and I were present in the large and otherwise empty sanctuary. Preaching in the sanctuary along with television cables and blank screens meant that I had to imagine you. I could only guess how you were responding to what I was saying.

Many of you were devoted to your engagement with the congregation through those years. Some of you even discovered us during that time. Others of you drifted or stopped attending services as much or at all, finding virtual worship lacking or different. I wanted to scream: *"Don't leave. Come back. We can do this. I can't do this alone. We need one another. I need you. I'm a person too."* At the same time, I understood. How could I blame you? And still, I missed you—missed us—so much.

When we re-gathered in person in the fall of 2021, I unconsciously did all I could to push that pain and grief away. "Don't make this about you, Reverend Rebecca. Stop feeling sorry for yourself; look what others have had to go through." I separated myself from the loss and carried on.

But back at home, I avoided that office, the space where we "did" church together throughout the pandemic.

Then, at the start of this year, my husband retired and offered me the larger office space in our home. "You should have it. I'll move into the smaller office," he said. I was grateful for the change and knew it would be good for me.

I also knew I needed to thank the space that had served as my office before I could change to a new space. I know the power of rituals, so I thought that thanking the space would allow me to feel complete and move on.

One morning two weeks ago, aware that I had been avoiding doing so, I opened the door to my home office. Georgia O'Keeffe's red and yellow-orange print hung on the wall. The blue chalice given to me decades ago by another congregation stood underneath it. The sun streamed into the small window, and the cold air condensed into dew, fogging the lower windowpanes.

I knelt on the floor and began to offer thanks for all that had happened in that space. The tears started, rivers of tears. As did happy and difficult memories, which came rushing back. I remained there on the floor until the release was complete, saying "thank you" again and again. After having that experience and now sharing it with you, I am complete.

"Sorrow is a sustained note in the song of being alive...Acknowledging this reality enables us to find our way into the grace that lies hidden in sorrow,"[26] writes Francis Weller, author of *The Wild Edge of Sorrow*.

Comparison has no place in sorrow. Thinking it does keeps us from sharing sorrow with one another. As long as I thought my pain was unjustified, it remained stuck inside of me.

When we think grief is bestowed unfairly on some people, we either feel guilty for our good fortune, or we keep away from the grieving person, fearing it may be contagious. We know that the other's grief runs the risk of touching our own grief that we have been trying to keep away.

Grief has been a lifelong companion of mine. I've come to honor her wisdom and treasure her gifts. Grief is part of life, to be embraced rather than feared. We grieve as deeply as we love.

I wish someone had taught me when I was younger how to be with grief and not let it overcome me. I am no longer afraid of the dark that often comes with grief and am at home in myself and my soul.

I hope to share some of that wisdom with you today. Many of you know more than I. According to Francis Weller, those who have learned to apprentice to sorrow and appreciate the lessons of grief are the elders. We have much to offer. These have been difficult lessons. Yet, the happiest people I know are those who know how to grieve.

I was stuck in disenfranchised grief for decades. It showed up as depression and feeling numb and disconnected from joy. I knew nothing better. I had none of the skills necessary to navigate my grief, but I have forgiven myself. Michael Lerner writes, "...great loss is wasted if we do not use it, over time, to discover what lies beyond great loss."[27]

Perhaps my grief is more radical than yours; perhaps it is not. Regardless of its origin and depth, at some point, we can all learn to find the good embedded in the earth of life, the likeness of sorrow and joy. We must till the earth in our own garden.

Our monthly ministry theme is *grief*. You might be wondering why. The reason for choosing grief is because to understand and realize those things that you have told me interest you most, such as peace, forgiveness, beauty, joy, theology, or community, we must know how to live with grief and process it, not as a one-time event to be endured, but as a part of life.

Much of today's sermon is based on the work of Francis Weller, who says this of grief:

For the most part, grief is not a problem to be solved, but a deep encounter with an essential experience of being human. The lack of courtesy and compassion surrounding grief is astonishing, reflecting an underlying fear and mistrust of this basic human experience. We must restore the healing ground of grief. We must find the courage, once again, to walk its wild edge.[28]

Grief is not something to be "gotten over." Grief is a messenger from our heart, a guide to what matters to us and a map through life's challenging and painful aspects. Contrary to what many of us are taught, grief is a friend of the soul. Grief work is soul work. It will lead us home to ourselves if we have the skills to be in relationship with it. "Grief work offers us a trail leading back to the vitality that is our birthright," writes Weller.[29]

He outlines five gates of grief, not "stages of grief." The first is *everything we love, we will lose.* When it comes to grief, people commonly think of the death of someone we love or the loss of something connected to our identity, such as our health, career, or marriage.

But grief doesn't stop there. The second gateway of grief includes *the places that have not known love.* These are the parts of ourselves or memories of which we are ashamed. They often show up as addictions, anxiety, or depression. Indigenous cultures call this *soul loss.* Carl Jung labeled these repressed or cut off parts of ourselves *complexes.* Internal Family Systems calls them exiles.

Buddhist teachers Pema Chödrön and Thich Nhat Hanh say that we must reclaim these parts of ourselves if we are to have peace. Weller writes "...it is in these outcasts, those parts of us that we have sent to the edges of awareness, that we will recover our true humanity."[30]

I have spent many years at this second gate. I go deeper into myself each time I venture there and return with untold treasures.

The third of the five gates is *the sorrows of the world*, or *anima mundi*, the soul of the world. This is where we are invited to process the grief over devastating planetary losses, climate destruction, and social injustices. This is where our pain goes when Tyre Nichols is killed or another language or animal species is lost, never to be spoken or seen again. We can be bearers of hope and good news only if we know how to process our grief. Unprocessed grief leaves us stuck in anger, overwhelm, or detachment.

I remember being with author and environmental activist Joanna Macy at a weeklong retreat in 2014. The information and communal rituals to help process grief were overwhelming to the point that I had to step away for large parts of the conference.

The last two gates of grief are *what we expected and did not receive* and *ancestral grief*. The fourth gate is deeply connected to our sense of belonging or worthiness and our sense of having a purpose. "Hidden within this gate lies our diminished experience of who we truly are."[31]

The fifth gate, *ancestral grief,* is the sorrow and unresolved loss we carry in our bodies from our ancestors; familial losses as well as those of the countries and people to which we are connected. This grief includes genocide and racism. The crimes of humanity are large.

Weller acknowledges that there are other gates of grief such as trauma: "Trauma always carries grief though not all grief carries trauma."[32]

Once we realize that grief is not something to get over or endure, we can be open to developing a new way of being in relationship with it. We can be open and curious rather than ashamed or afraid. We can use grief to connect with our truest self and be present with others. We can allow our grief to equalize us, open us, and help us bond in our common humanity.

Creating a relationship with grief requires having space and patience, solitude and community, and support and rituals. The process is not to be hurried. It is not a 1-2-3 process. It is deep soul work and an essential part of spiritual community.

Each of you should have received a journal on entering the church. I invite you to use it throughout February to journal, add photographs, or doodle. It is a container for your process this month.

Hold your journal in your hand. Place your dominant hand over the bow and your nondominant hand on top. Take a breath and close your eyes.

Bring to your mind the part of grief you want to explore this month. It may be a specific loss, one of the gates, or something else. Sit with this for a moment. Let it know you are interested in its gifts and in learning how to be with it. (pause)

As you are ready, gently untie your bow.

To end with words of Francis Weller:

> Grief...isn't there to take us hostage, but instead to reshape us in some fundamental way...capable of living in the creative tension between grief and gratitude.[33] Every loss we experience in our lifetime has the capacity to deepen us, to widen the channel of soul life flowing into us.[34]

So may we move together.

Part Four

Spirituality

13

The Power and the Possibility
of Liminality

August 25, 2019

It was time for me to go to the hospital and receive medical care. I had been dealing with searing pain in my throat and diaphragm for seven days and it was only getting worse. My dentist, who had put me on an antibiotic for what he believed was an infection, had told me the pain should be gone in two days. He would need to do further testing if antibiotics didn't do the trick.

I had been hoping that antibiotics would treat the infection, thereby eliminating the need for further medical procedures. The pain was increasing, and I was afraid of the endoscopy I thought might be necessary. My thoughts were racing. I had never had an endoscopy. Would it hurt? Today is Saturday; what if I can't preach tomorrow?

As I sat debating whether to go to the emergency room, I realized that I was once again in a space of liminality. Liminality, or the "in between times," are the times in our lives when what *has been* is no longer true, and what *will be* is not yet known. In this situation I was no longer the person who had never experienced this kind of throat-to-sternum pain that felt like a fire moving down my esophagus and landing in my chest. I now knew what this kind of pain felt like, and yet, I did not know what was to come.

Some people call these times of liminality the hallways of life. We all go through them. Some liminal times last a short while and others can exist for a number of years. Regardless of the duration, the key to liminality is that something that had been true is no longer, and what will be true is not yet known. Inherently, liminality includes loss, even when we choose the change and know it is right.

Liminal space is a term used in anthropology as well as psychology and theology. It is that time or times between realities. It can be a scary, lonely, and confusing time. It can also be an exciting, creative, and hopeful time. Regardless, it is a deeply human experience and one that we all experience a multitude of times over the course of years. All of our lives have litter, and layers. Stanley Kunitz writes about liminality in his poem "The Layers."

> *I have walked through many lives,*
> *some of them my own,*
> *and I am not who I was....*
> *How shall the heart be reconciled*
> *to its feast of losses?...*
> *In my darkest night,*
> *when the moon was covered*
> *and I roamed through wreckage,*
> *a nimbus-clouded voice*
> *directed me:*

> *"Live in the layers,*
> *not on the litter."*

Kunitz, born in Worcester, Massachusetts, in 1905, was the poet laureate of the United States in 1974 as well as Consultant in Poetry to the Library of Congress in the year 2000. His life was full of loss and liminal times. Six weeks before Stanley was born, his father went bankrupt and committed suicide. His mother, who was Lithuanian, remarried and opened a dry goods store, after which she declared bankruptcy. His stepfather died of a heart attack when Stanley was fourteen.

> *How shall the heart be reconciled*
> *to its feast of losses?*

Kunitz earned his bachelor's and master's degrees from Harvard. He was denied, however, when he applied to study at Harvard for his doctorate. He was told it would not go over well with the other students to be taught by a Jew. Later in his life, Kunitz was denied conscientious objector status in World War II and was sent instead to serve in active duty.

> *In my darkest night,*
> *when the moon was covered*
> *and I roamed through wreckage,*
> *a nimbus-clouded voice*
> *directed me:*
> *"Live in the layers,*
> *not on the litter."*

Though one of the most influential poets of our time, Kunitz's journey in publishing poetry was not an easy one. Only three volumes of poetry were published in the first thirty years of his writing.

We realize, when we explore some of the history of this great poet, that Kunitz writes his poem "The Layers" from a place of experience, of truth. He speaks from deep experiences with liminality when he writes of having many lives in his own life, struggling to make peace with his losses, and being inspired to live in the layers, not the litter.

Each of us is living in some or many liminal spaces. When seasons change, we share in the liminality of the end of summer and the start of autumn. We may take a child or grandchild to college. We may start a new job, or we may be preparing to leave a job. We may be wondering what is happening in our world and what is going to be happening in the days and months to come. We may be lost. We may almost be found. We may be on the edge of what is still unknown.

Our lives are in constant transition; all of our life is indeed liminal. William Butler Yeats wrote: "How many times a person lives and dies between the two eternities."[35]

In liminal times we may look to something, someone, or anything outside of ourselves to tell us what to do or to relieve the pain.

Liminality is inherently uncomfortable, ambiguous, and uncertain. Unless we are conscious of it, our instinctual reaction to this kind of discomfort will be to run and find ground or safety as quickly as we can.

Living consciously, without reactivity and with a presence of mind in this space of liminality, requires a lot from us. To be conscious and non-reactive requires spiritual and emotional skills. We need to know how to find ground inside of ourselves when there may be none around us. Being present means that we remain open when we want to close and choose to be a non-anxious presence in the midst of turmoil and fear.

These skills are not taught in the classroom or work environments. Being able to live well in liminal space is not about knowledge or intellect. In fact, our minds can be obstacles to receiving the gifts of liminality.

There are gifts to this liminal space, but we must be open to recognizing them. Some of the gifts include developing spiritual maturity and deeper compassion. Times of liminality can help us to learn how to live more humbly, develop softness, and understand the power of vulnerability. During times of liminality, we realize the importance of acts of kindness, small and large.

Being able to live well during times of "no more and not yet" often demands that we let go of what used to be, including beliefs we held as "truths" and "conclusions," as Tolstoy called them.[36] We also must be able to sit with hard feelings and discern when and where action is necessary.

I sum up the life skills necessary to be at peace with liminality with two mantras: "Do the next right thing" and "Let it be."

Do the next right thing. When we live in times of uncertainty, like liminal space, it is best to focus on right now, not on the horizon. Focusing on the present helps us to live in just *this* moment, knowing we will respond to the next moment when it comes.

Another time of liminality was when I was a new mother with an infant baby. I remember feeling so overwhelmed. I would walk around the house with the burping blanket over my shoulder, my baby having just fallen asleep, and wonder, "What now?" When I called a dear friend to ask how to best handle having an infant, she asked how long it had been since I had taken a shower. When I answered, "I don't know, probably a week," she said, "Take a shower."

"Do the next right thing."

Doing the next right thing during times of change or loss often requires that we cancel plans, take it easy on ourselves, and allow ourselves the space to grieve. Doing nothing is often the next right thing, especially during liminal times.

Which brings me to my second mantra for liminality: **Let it be.** There is incredible power and strength in being able to let things be. Being able to let things be helps us maintain perspective and trust that the discomfort we feel during times of liminality is healing. Liminality is creative potential and energy at work. Letting things be is the wisdom we have when we know that there is nothing to be fixed, and time cannot be made to move any faster than it is moving. The Serenity Prayer reinforces this power of acceptance in its familiar words: *God grant me the serenity to accept the things I cannot change, courage to change the things I can, and the wisdom to know the difference.*

In his book *Transitions*, William Bridges, a leading expert on change, writes of his wife's premature death in her mid-fifties. Bridges recalls one night when his wife was in a lot of pain and things were particularly bad. He was sitting beside the bed watching her struggle to breathe when she said to him, "This positive thinking stuff is crap. But then so is negative thinking. They both cover up reality—which is that we just don't know what is going to happen. That's the reality we have to live with."[37] Bridges goes on to say, "It is easy to see why people take refuge in optimism or pessimism. They both give you an answer. But the truth is that we just don't know. What a hard truth that is!"[38] "Let it Be."

When we don't let it be—in other words, when we act prematurely or out of a need to know the answer before its time—we run the risk of cutting off creative possibilities. We jump to a place called *safety*, and we miss the space called *possibility*. I know. It's an old habit I am trying to break.

Consider the liminal places that you are in or have been in. Reflect upon the lives and friends that you have left behind, the layers that make up your life, and the feast of losses that your heart must reconcile.

Ask yourself:

What am I leaving behind?

What layers are there to carry me?

What is my next right step?

And how can I let it be?

This liminality—it's a human thing. When we find ourselves in times of liminality, *let's do the next thing, love ourselves and others, take heart, and let it be.*

14
Quiet
May 10, 2020

I come from a family of musicians as well as writers, academics, and farmers. Singing camp songs, discussing theater, and debating politics are fundamental to the Bryan heritage. With all the music in our family, it was an "outsider" who helped me to make the connection to my favorite music. This outsider was my daughter's new boyfriend, Alex.

One day, Alex and I were waiting for my daughter to return from an errand and were enjoying a few minutes of casual conversation. Knowing that he was a musician in his free time, I asked Alex what his favorite type of music was. He answered immediately, "Rock and roll," then turned to me and asked in return. "What is your favorite type of music?"

I sat for a moment and then answered honestly. "Silence."

It was an epiphany and a homecoming at the same time. Silence *is* my favorite form of music; it always has been.

Negative space, or silence, has a long history in music. Music critic Corinna da Fonseca-Wollheim writes this of silence in music, "What unites music's negative spaces—whether they are designed for comedy, drama, or mysticism—is their power to propel the listener from the role of passive consumer to active participant."[39] Examples of such uses of silence are seen in Japanese Dotaku bells, monks' silence, symphonies, operas, and Baroque music.

We see the influence and power of silence in music as early as the third century when Dotaku bells were made in Japan. These unusual bells have no clapper and thus can make no sound. Some believe they were used in rituals to bless crops.

Monks use silence in their call and responses for morning prayers. They will convene and break into two lines and stand across from each other in between the buildings in their monasteries. One line of the monks sings, and the other line waits until the sound is received to return the call. The silence in between the first monk's sound and the other monk's reply is part of the music.

Monteverdi writes about music and silence in his opera, *L'Orfeo*, and early Baroque music uses rests in a literal way. Beethoven used silence in stunning and varied ways in his "Eroica" symphony, including mystical silence, dramatic silence, and explosive silence, this last being the unexpected pause that follows a series of louder and louder music. Nineteenth-century music, including Tchaikovsky's Sixth Symphony and Brahms' Third Symphony, used liminal silence and quiet.

In recent times, we have John Cage's 1952 performance of silence in Woodstock, New York, and Miles Davis' use of silence in jazz.

Of course, I didn't know any of that when I fell in love with silence as music. I just knew that music and silence are two experiences where I connect with the divine. And when you put them together, it's heavenly.

Aldous Huxley wrote, "After silence, that which comes nearest to expressing the inexpressible is music."[40] I wholeheartedly agree.

And that "outsider" I told you about? Well, he's as close as a person can be to being part of our family, although he loves Queen, and I love Quiet.

15
The Axis Mundi:
Its Role in Mindfulness and
Across Disciplines

October 15, 2023

I first heard the term "axis mundi" from Reverend Craig Barnes this summer while at the Chautauqua Institute. He described it using T.S. Eliot's phrase, "the still point of the turning world." My ears immediately perked up, as did my heart. I know that place, I thought to myself. It's home.

Rev. Barnes went on to talk a bit more about the axis mundi and how it is understood in cultures and relations across time as a symbol of the connection between heaven and earth. A connection between heaven and earth? I thought. I need that. I had always believed that regardless of what we thought about an afterlife, we could all help create more peace and love, or heaven, on Earth. My curiosity piqued; I left with a desire to know more. What I learned fascinated me.

German-born spiritual teacher Eckhart Tolle calls this axis mundi the *vertical dimension*. He explains that most of us are more accustomed to living in the *horizontal plane* as experienced when we talk with others, watch the news, or focus on our daily tasks. Connections made on the horizontal axis are necessary and can be good; the interconnection with the vertical axis, the eternal home within us all, the axis mundi, is *also* important.

Tolle says, "You enter the vertical dimension as you become present. As you become present, the stream of thinking subsides and is replaced with awareness. You know you are, but that's it and that's all you need to know."[41]

In astronomy, axis mundi is the Latin term for the axis of Earth between the celestial poles. Elsewhere, it is called the "Tree of Life," the center of the Earth, the world axis, or the world pillar. It is portrayed in da Vinci's painting, *Vitruvian Man*. Mayan culture described it as a cosmic mountain. In Japan, this is Mount Fuji. In the Old Testament, it was Mount Zion. It was Mount Olympus in Greek mythology and the Black Hills from the Sioux.[42]

Some cultures visualize the axis mundi as a column or pillar, while others see the axis mundi in the image of a tree. Hindus call it the fig tree in the Upanishads, while in Buddhism it is the Bodhi Tree under which Siddhartha Gautama gained enlightenment. It has been explained that the tree is under- stood to be the "reconciliation of macrocosm and microcosm"[43] or "as above, so below." To me this means that truth is found in the largest and smallest of experiences, parts of nature, and expressions of truth.

Axis mundi is contemplated in most of the world religions. It is incorporated into architecture, reflected in nature, and woven into many cultures, including for example, Greek civilization. Axis Mundi is interconnected into a variety of disciplines and world views.

It is interesting to study how the axis mundi shows up in various religions and cultures. The real questions are, of course, *Why does this matter? What does it have to do with interconnectedness and mindfulness?* And if it does, *how do we find it for ourselves?*

It matters, according to Craig Barnes and T.S. Eliot among other theologians and poets, because all people revolve around something. Our lives can revolve around fear, concern around external matters, or a person. What we revolve around, which can be part of our conscious or unconscious belief systems, can be inherited or intentional. Belief systems, including our axis mundi, can be helpful or not so helpful.

The challenge with revolving our lives around anything other than truth—including fear, people's opinions, or our outward success—is that all but the truth will eventually fail us or leave us. Change, or truth, is the only constant. The axis mundi is the place within us that will never leave us—as long as we are alive, at least.

Our internal axis mundi is always present, accessible, and unblemished. It is the resonance of our true self, or what some call our soul. The axis mundi is also called the deeper self, no-self, and transcendent self. Internal Family Systems, a branch of psychology which sees humans as a web of interconnected parts, calls it the "Self" with a capital S. The key is to be able to access our axis mundi, become conscious of it, connect to it, and then return to it again and again.

Paradoxically, the deeper and more genuinely we connect with our internal axis mundi, the more we are connected to others and the world around us. The difference is that we are not connected out of fear or inappropriate insecurity, as we are when our sense of self revolves around outer conditions or people.

I didn't always know that I had an axis mundi or how to connect with it. I didn't believe there was a place within me, or a part of me, that no one and nothing could ever harm. Finding this place of centeredness has been a decades-long process, with many paths leading to the ultimate connection. It is well worth all it took to get to this place.

A turning point in my own journey came four years ago. I injured my back and needed to take a break from Hatha and power yoga. A yoga practitioner for over thirty years, I had never explored Kundalini yoga. The practice, which includes breath-work and the use of sound, mantra, and mudras or hand gestures, didn't burn many calories, and my revolution at that time still involved imposed beliefs about body and health. But the gift that my injured back offered was that I had no choice; if I wanted to practice yoga, it was going to have to be Kundalini yoga, at least temporarily. I started and never left the practice!

Through consistent practice of this type of yoga, I found my voice and learned to sing and connect with my axis mundi. Sound, in my case, through the Sikh tradition and language of Gurmukhi, led me to my inner axis mundi. Sound and singing are now a central tenet of my spiritual practices. The sounds and words quickly connect me to my home inside, my axis mundi.

Sound is certainly not the only path to connect with our axis mundi. Athletes can find it in their sport, gardeners in gardening, and others in mindful stillness. Some people have mystical experiences where the veil of illusion is dropped; they experience the interconnectedness of all existence, and feelings of awe and mystery abound. Great joy, laughter, and play can all connect us to the still point within us. Ironically people also can experience this stillness during times of tragedy or crisis. "Somehow I knew things were going to be okay, regardless of the outcome," a woman told me as she was undergoing treatment for cancer. People share how time stood still, or that they felt a peace that made no sense in the face of tragedy.

Whatever or however it happens, accessing our axis mundi requires us to override or set down our thinking, so that we may experience this place of wholeness and interconnection. As we detach from others and all we believe we know, we find our home, the still point in a turning world, as Eliot said. We realize there is nothing that must be done, and from there, so much happens. Once we find that still point within our axis mundi, we have an ever-available place of calm. We begin to live—truly live—and be present. We feel our place in the interconnected world of which we are an essential and beautiful part, and we are home.

We have found the still point within—the axis mundi—from which all goodness flows.

16
The Expectation and Promise of Peace
Christmas Eve 2022

Peace.

Peace is not the absence of challenges. Peace is not the outcome of everything happening the way we think it should.

Peace is not an award and isn't given to those who work the hardest or those who most often do as they are told to do.

Peace is within us. It is a choice to not let the challenges, the difficulties, the broken promises or dreams get us down. It is a commitment to serenity against all odds.

Do you think Mary expected to give birth in a stable? I bet she expected a Hilton. After all, she and Joseph were doing what they were told was right. They were paying their taxes, following their lineage as people of King David. I imagine they were hungry, tired, and scared. How could they not have been? In addition to doing what they were expected to do, they were also breaking all kinds of cultural norms. Unmarried, expecting a child. Imagine the judgments...

Have you ever done what was expected of you, played by the rules, treated people right, paid your dues, and found that life failed to deliver the reward to you? I know I have. And did the lack of reward bring you down or lead you to resentment or fear? Did it rob you of your peace?

Did you expect a Hilton and find yourself at a stable? And if so, have you realized yet that the promised gifts of playing by the rules, being who people tell you to be, and following a script that is not your authentic expression never lead to peace?

The promise of peace lies within us. No one and no circumstances have the power to rob us of that, and if anyone or anything taught you differently, I am sorry.

But there is time.

It is always possible to choose peace, to focus on the stillness, and to rest in that place of goodness within us, even when our expectations are not met, even when things are hard. Especially when things are hard.

Peace, my friends, is an unearned gift. It is a companion, a friend to accompany us throughout our lives. Peace is one of the surprising guests that shows up in the darkest and most vulnerable of hours, when someone is aging or dying, or when we are afraid.

Peace comes, often not in ways we expect it, but rather in surprising, unexpected places and conditions—if we are open, if we are willing to enter in.

In his Nobel Peace Prize acceptance speech, Costa Rican activist Oscar Arias Sánchez said, "Peace is not a matter of prizes or trophies. It is not the product of a victory or command. It has no finishing line, no final deadline, no fixed definition of achievement."[44]

Peace is a way of life. It is a choice, it is strong, and it is enduring.

This I promise you.

Take peace.

Part Five

Justice

17

Love at the Center: Politics and Religion

September 15, 2024

I chose this year's annual ministry theme of Truth last April, a time when many of you were nervous—about the future of democracy, the real and present danger of rising authoritarianism, and the increasing division within our country.

Person after person asked me and each other: *How do we respond to all of this as Unitarian Universalists? What does our faith call us to do? Can we love people who harm others and prioritize their personal agendas and rhetoric over human rights? And are they people of worth and dignity?* People were nervous and at a loss as to how to respond and were turning to their faith for answers.

I soon realized that not only were people fearful of what was happening in our country and for the future of democracy, but they were being forced to look deeply at our Unitarian Universalist principles—at the worth and dignity of every person, for example—and ask if these principles still held true.

I remember talking with someone and asking if they felt that elected officials, past and present, who were committing some of these most terrible acts, were forgivable. "I don't know," the person said. "It feels so hard." Where is the hope for the future if these officials are not forgivable? I asked. We still refer to that conversation.

These are deep existential questions.

I took seriously the questions you were asking and decided we would journey *together* asking tough questions: *What is true? How do we respond faithfully as individuals and a spiritual community committed to love, peace, and justice? How do truth and bravery connect? How do other religions understand truth? What is truth in our personal lives?*

We will go deep into those questions and more this year. But we need to start today by talking about politics and religion. Because the situation is pressing and the threats of what may happen in our country are real.

It is time to talk about the intersection and interconnection of religion and politics. Before I continue, let me make it clear why I am bringing politics to the pulpit. It is not to misuse the pulpit, or to push a political agenda in the name of religion. Nor do I speak of politics to affirm to us that we are right, or to, in any way, further divide people, one against another.

Like Mahatma Ghandi, I speak of politics because religion cannot be separated from politics. Both have to do with power: the power to unite, empower, and ensure equity and safety for all people, and the power to diminish, control, and kill in the name of personal agendas or advancement.

Whenever either politics or religion are used to hurt people and our Earth, and to dehumanize and divide people and create conditions and systems that result in fear and destruction, we cannot be silent, not even in the name of separation of church and state.

When politics or religion privileges those who have historically been in power and blatantly lie, when politics is used to oppress, when politics and its people create rules that are killing our Earth and its creatures, those of us with religious values that contradict those actions must step up to do what we can to stop those crimes.

Years ago, Reverend Bertrand Steeves, minister of this congregation, stood up against antisemitism. It was a political action coming out of religious values. When we housed an Afghan family of refugees, or human paroles, as they were designated upon their arrival, we were taking political action based on our religious values.

So, too, are we taking political action based on our religious values when we hang our Black Lives Matter banner and pass an 8th Principle that specifically states our commitment to work to end the oppression of Black people, and all forms of oppression. When nearly 200 FRSUU members and friends recently signed their names on an ad, published in *The Daily News*, stating that we oppose all forms of violence against women, including on billboards, we were taking political action based on our religious values.

The truth is that there are times when you cannot separate politics from religion without, in my opinion, being sacrilegious or hypocritical. Now is one of those times.

Unitarian Universalism is a religious tradition long steeped in engagement with social issues. We are a church where service is our prayer and always will be.

We are in a time when silence is not only complacency but is also doing harm. I stand here not to ask you to vote for a person, but rather to vote for our democracy, human rights, and for elected officials who respect the rule of law. To vote for people who work to ensure that all people are safe and given the care they need, and that we work together as global partners to respond to climate destruction in the most effective and immediate ways possible. This is no time to be silent.

We must bring the feelings you experience here in church into the streets. We must care for our nation and her people and all sentient beings as we care for one another here. We must open our hearts wide enough to know and feel the truth that until everyone is free, none of us is free.

At the same time, we must act in ways aligned with our religious values. This means we act without disdain for others. Disdain does not foster shared understanding, it does not build bridges where there is divide, and it certainly does nothing to change minds. When was the last time someone who called you an idiot or yelled in your face changed your mind about anything?

We cannot be silent, and we cannot return evil for evil. Casting our fear and anger onto others harms us as much as the other and interferes with the potential of creating common ground. The high road is to continue to work for what we believe in and strive to love our neighbors in the highest sense of the word.

All Republicans are not stupid, and all Democrats are not enlightened. We are all people, and here at FRS we are people committed to justice, compassion, and equity for all people, living creatures, and the Earth. We don't know other people's stories; we don't know who they are or what formed their opinions.

Do we need to learn how to challenge our anger and our fear? Yes. Does it help when we dehumanize and antagonize others who think differently? No. It *is* helpful when we channel our anger and conviction into positive action, and this action need not be large. It just needs to be constructive.

Don't let others rob you of your dignity or inner peace. Turn off the television after a while. Work to get out the vote or thank people who are doing that. Return to this sanctuary, so that we can love you when you are frightened, hear you when you are angry, and make space for you to return to the best version of yourself.

It is natural to get angry and feel afraid. The spiritual path calls us to be good stewards of those feelings. This means using those feelings to propel us forward, or processing and releasing them without harming others, so we can be stewards of peace and goodwill as we work for justice.

My friends, we are often self-righteous and quick to point out the faults in others, instead of understanding what those faults in others touch off in us and learning how to respond to them appropriately.

It is hard to feel powerless and afraid. It is hard to feel rage, and there are many, many people who have lived with those feelings of powerlessness, fear, and rage for generations. The historically marginalized and oppressed... We might learn a lot from them.

We can start by learning their stories. Learn how Sojourner Truth's faith in her God got her through all her struggles, or how the person down your street who can't afford to buy groceries still has ways to help their children feel confident and good about who they are.

Our feelings of powerlessness over everything that is occurring have us experiencing base emotions that many people in the world have had to negotiate for a very long time and still do today—including right here today in this sanctuary. We are here right now with others who know what it means to be unsafe, to have little power, or to be silenced. We can learn from each other.

An essential part of the spiritual life is truly learning to put yourself in others' shoes, which we cannot do if we don't know others. That means we must listen well and hear others' stories and learn more about them as people. Some of us are fortunate to be able to do this in personal relationships. We can also do this by being intentional about what we read and listen to on television, in news or in podcasts. When we live from this place of openness and curiosity, we begin to see that the ways in which events affect any of us are not the same.

Take, for example, the heinous and hurtful lies, spoken on a recent political stage, that immigrants eat other people's pets. This is so extreme that some people say it's funny. It's not funny if you are an immigrant. For immigrants, these untrue statements are scary. Rather than post a meme, reach out to immigrants you know or send a letter or card to the Haitian-American Public Health Initiatives, who work with Haitians on the ground and in shel-ters in Mattapan.

With all of the challenges and stressors of this time, we can still choose to help transform these uncertain and frightening times into the beginning of a new way of relating to one another, one in which we truly come to understand and respect one another. This kind of shared understanding is built on sacred ground, where all people are worthy, and all voices deserve to be heard and respected.

"The UU minister Jim Brewer...reminds us: 'Freedom demands responsibility to others and life.' Being a UU is about much more than the opinions and beliefs you hold; it is about the way you *live* every day. Our tradi-tion has always affirmed that true religion is *about deeds, not creeds.* UUs are fond of saying, 'Don't tell me what you believe, show me how you live.' As one minister pointedly put it in his sermon title, 'If being a Unitarian Universalist were against the law, would there be enough evidence to convict you?'"[45]

My friends, as we move forward through the days and weeks ahead, may we do so as people of faith, acting in ways that align with our values of truth, justice, and equity for all. May we be brave enough to know people. May we focus on values and refrain from disdain, remembering that everyone has their stories and that for any of us to be liberated, we must all be liberated. May we return here for sanctuary, work for the good of all, and return no evil for evil. Regardless of who wins the election on November 5, we have work to do, and we will not turn back.

18
Open Our Hearts
Christmas Eve 2021

The year was 1967. It was the year the first heart transplant took place, the first ATM was made public, and the Public Broadcasting System was incorporated.

It was also the year that The Beatles recorded their world-famous album, *Sergeant Pepper's Lonely Hearts Club Band*. The album went on to achieve "Diamond" status by selling eleven million copies, far surpassing the requisite ten million sales mark. The album's top hits included "When I'm Sixty-Four" and "Lucy in the Sky with Diamonds."[46]

The songs, however, are not the part of the story I want to highlight tonight. The part of the story I want to focus on has to do with a stranger whom Paul McCartney welcomed in.

The story goes that The Beatles were preparing to record this famous album when a homeless person, claiming to be Jesus, came to the door of the studio. He asked if he could come in and watch the recording. Paul said yes and let him in.

After sharing a cup of tea, Paul went back to recording and the man sat silently in the back of the recording studio for the entire session, never uttering a word. He left at the end of the day, and the band never saw him again.

Later, Paul was asked, of course, why he let the man into the studio and whether he really thought the person was Jesus. Paul replied, "Well, he probably isn't. But if he was, I'm not going to be the one to turn him away."[47]

That may sound funny or endearing, but I ask you, and I ask all of us, "What would we do?" What would we do if a homeless or "otherized" person showed up at the door of our home, our office, our church, claiming to be Jesus? Would we let them in and pour them a cup of tea?

Well, that's what many people in Newburyport and the surrounding towns are doing. Churches including St. Paul's Episcopal Church, West Newbury Congregational Church, and our church are opening their doors to provide temporary housing to Afghan refugee families while permanent housing is found. And it doesn't stop there. The First Parish Newbury Food Pantry offers food every Friday to hundreds of people of all ages. The list of such places is long and includes the YWCA, Emmaus Incorporated, Jeanne Geiger Crisis Center, Pegasus House, Link House, Open Table, Habitat for Humanity, and many others.

This is critical work, not because it saves needy people, but because it saves us all. Welcoming the stranger and opening our hearts requires bravery, faith, and trust.

Welcoming the stranger and opening our hearts requires

bravery to walk into the unknown, the uncomfortable, the dark, where no step is laid out in advance.

It requires faith that what we do, however seemingly small, matters. Our time matters. Our attention matters. Our love matters.

Welcoming the stranger and opening our hearts requires trust, which means it requires community, where we lay down the burden of trying to live alone, isolated, or disconnected. Community is where we choose to claim our belonging and where we choose to work side by side, addressing the many needs of this world. Community is where we choose to celebrate every step we take toward good with others who also care about these things.

Welcoming the stranger and opening our hearts is an orientation and way of living. It is a spiritual practice that Jesus taught.

Poet Amanda Gorman, in her poem "Practice Makes People," writes this:

> The making of plans
> When this is over,
> The We can't wait,
> Really our knuckles rapping
> Against the future, sounding
> Out what lies beneath its hull.
> But tomorrow isn't revealed,
> Rather rendered, refined. Wrought.
> Remember that fate isn't fought
> Against. It is fought for. Again
> & again...[48]

These are challenging times, my friends, increasingly so with the coronavirus Omicron variant and the cold winter months. What *is* happening? What *will* happen?

Remember that 1967 was also a difficult year. So was the year Jesus is said to have been born, some two thousand years ago. And yet, even in the difficulty, the uncertainty, and the challenges of the times, a stranger was welcomed—into a recording studio and into a stable. There, a stranger became a friend.

May we all welcome the stranger, open our hearts, and invite in the miracles that await such acts of faith.

19
The Invention of Air

December 9, 2018

That ideas should freely spread from one to another over the globe, for the moral and mutual instruction of men, and improvement of man's condition, seems to have been peculiarly and benevolently designed by nature, when she made them, like fire, expansible over all space without lessening their density at any point, and like the air in which we breathe, move, and have our physical being, incapable of confinement of exclusive appropriation.
Thomas Jefferson[49]

The quote above from the book *The Invention of Air* by Steven Johnson made me smile and immediately inspired me to read further. Not only was Jefferson one of our country's founding fathers, and, like so many other founders, connected to Unitarianism, his words reflect one of my key beliefs about creativity: that *creativity is not a solo practice.*

Even people who appear to create alone do not. Ideas are rooted in—connected to—other ideas. Ideas become original when we imbue them with who we are, not because we create them out of nothing.

The 7th Principle of our Unitarian Universalist faith says this: "We covenant to affirm and promote respect for the interdependent web of all existence of which we are a part." Reverend Forrest Gilmore writes, "Our 7th Principle, respect for the interdependent web of all existence, is a glorious statement. Yet we make a profound mistake when we limit it to merely an environmental idea. It is so much more. It is our response to the great dangers of both individualism and oppression."[50]

Jefferson, a contemporary and comrade of Joseph Priestly and John Adams, among others, was a polymath, or a person of far-reaching and deep knowledge across many disciplines. Joseph Priestly, a founder of Unitarianism as well as the early years of our country, was also a polymath, as was John Adams. In fact, so were many, if not most, educated men of that time. Learning across disciplines was the norm and as natural as, well, slavery and the oppression of women.

I reference slavery and oppression of women not to be funny. Rather, I must not romanticize. If I am to focus on the gifts and many important contributions that these white men made, I must also acknowledge that it was not Utopia. Oppression, slavery, and violence were all rampant and normal during this time period.

Steven Johnson describes how learning, discovering, and creating happened in the mid-18th and early-19th centuries: "... vital fields of intellectual achievement cannot be cordoned off from one another and relegated to the specialist. The protagonists of this story lived in a climate where ideas flowed easily between the realms of politics, philosophy, religions and science."[51]

The protagonists he is referring to are specifically Joseph Priestly, John Adams, and Thomas Jefferson. More broadly, the book includes a group of men from London who were known as "The Club of Honest Whigs," dubbed so by Benjamin Franklin. These men, steeped in medicine, theology, music, electrostatics, and politics, were some of London's most "celebrated heretics."[52] Are we surprised that an impressive number of them were also early proponents and believers of Unitarianism?

While we may be more familiar with Adams and Jefferson as our country's second and third presidents, Joseph Priestly may be less familiar. In addition to founding the first Unitarian Association in America along with Theophilus Lindsey in 1774, he discovered many things. His most well-known discovery was oxygen, and his favorite discovery was carbonated water.

Contrary to most experiments today, which are protected and held in the highest confidence, Priestly and his colleagues came together to hear about what the others were learning. Priestly was even described as a "compulsive sharer."[53] He wrote volumes of books on his experiments, describing every step, question, and lesson that went along with them.

He was not alone in this practice. Benjamin Franklin was also committed to sharing his experiments and learnings as they progressed. In a letter to a friend written in 1753, Franklin said, "...even short Hints, and imperfect Experiments...being communicated, have sometimes a good Effect, in exciting the attention of the Ingenious to the Subject...you are at liberty to communicate this paper with whomever you please; it being of more Importance that Knowledge should increase..."[54] than that a person's reputation should grow in stature.

How many of us grew up this way? How many of us were taught to set aside competition and embrace collaboration? To celebrate the continued growth and evolution of one of your ideas as others use it. Or did you learn, as I did, that there were rewards, rankings, and honors to be earned. "Taking credit where credit is due." Now this, like most things, can be overdone. When people are operating in an oppressive system that does not allow their creativity to flourish or their voice to be heard, they must stand up and claim their ideas, inventions, and words.

Imagine, though, living in a system where all voices are equal —an organization, culture, or congregation where all people— Black people, Latinx, women, young people—*all* people have input. Within this system, people can share freely, create and work together, and celebrate one another's flourishing. In this collaborative creative culture, people use words like "we" much more frequently than "I" or "you."

When people live in systems that value competition instead of collaboration, inequality, oppression, and hierarchy are inevitable. To continue perpetuating such a system, people must forget the truth that we are all interconnected. To believe the lie that we are not connected, people must believe that we are separate and independent. Living with that lie, people treat each other unequally; they suppress, oppress, and deny. This kind of treatment traumatizes people.

Traumatized people, full of pain and rage, believe that they too are separate, so they turn to things outside of themselves for relief. Addiction becomes normal. Without help, traumatized people either turn against themselves or against others. Traumatized people do not trust others. They instinctively turn away and are not able to create in collaborative ways. And so the cycle continues until oppression, separation, and pain are the norm.

We can choose differently. We—FRSUU—can be a place, a spiritual community of liberal religious people, where people can come to heal. We can be a place where we create, work, and worship together, in ways that are based on equity, collaboration, and mutual respect. We can do that. We *are* doing that. We have a lot more ground to cover, and we will—because we are committed to our principles, to each other, and to the world around us.

Our founding fathers—John Adams, Thomas Jefferson, Joseph Priestly, and the like—promoted good that lives on and continues to guide our world today. They learned well together, across disciplines. Yet because they did not include diversity in people, the ultimate source of true creativity, hierarchy and oppression ruled, and creativity became more of a solo act than a communal transformation.

Transformation is possible. People who have been traumatized, marginalized, and silenced can recover. In that recovery, they can learn to trust. They can find a joy they never dreamed possible. They can find a community of creativity and love that allows them to fully express who they are. They can. I know, because I did.

20

The Work of Lifetimes

January 24, 2021

Whose pain is it?

I was lying in Shavasana, or corpse pose, at the end of yoga class, when the veil between the conscious and unconscious was lifted. In that moment I was gifted with an epiphany that liberated me. I had been struggling for months with guilt, anxiety, and confusion about my choices with my career and motherhood. I knew I was blessed to have choices, and yet they were still difficult.

At the tender age of twenty-seven, I was choosing a "both-and" approach to motherhood and my career, working part time and having significant time at home with my baby. Staying at home sounded great, and I expected it to feel great, but balancing work and motherhood didn't. Instead, it felt like the weight of the world was on me as I struggled to overcome these feelings of guilt. I kept asking myself, "What is wrong with you that you want to work and don't want to be home with your new baby all the time?"

And then in that yoga class, I was set free. The realization came to me by means of a thought... *Whose pain is this?*

As soon as the thought came, I knew it was my mother's pain I was carrying, not mine. I'm guessing my mother, as a divorced woman, felt guilty about working, even though she didn't have a choice. Knowing the pain that she lived in for all her life, it was also clear to me that she never forgave herself for that, and many other things. Her guilt and unresolved pain were passed on to me, as legitimately as her genes.

"The deep connection between personal liberation and social transformation is increasingly clear,"[55] write the authors of *Radical Dharma: Talking Race, Love, and Liberation*. It is difficult, if not impossible, to work for justice for other people in life-affirming, creative, and collaborative ways, guided by love, if we live imprisoned in resentment, trauma, or other states of unforgiveness. We *can* do the work of social justice without also engaging in personal healing, but often it then comes from places of obligation, ego, or vengeance.

Living with unresolved personal burdens and pain results in anxiety, depression, and unhealthy anger among other things, as well as a decreased ability to trust, connect, and stay embodied. When we approach societal change from those places, we are not bringing our whole, integrated, healed selves, and therefore we run the risk of causing further harm, or burning out.

The authors of *Radical Dharma* recognize this when they talk about the success of the current movement for the liberation of Black lives, and how it "must be articulated by and inextricably linked to an embodied personal liberation."[56]

We witnessed the same need in response to the Holocaust, so poignantly displayed by Holocaust survivor and forgiveness advocate Eva Kor, may she rest in peace. On the 50th anniversary of the liberation of Auschwitz in 1995, she stood in the presence of Dr. Munch who had operated the gas chambers, and after he read his statement of truth about these crimes, she forgave him. "As I did that," she said, "I felt a burden of pain was lifted from me. I was no longer in the grip of hate; I was finally free."[57]

This forgiveness and personal liberation, however—and this is so important—did not happen in a vacuum. Kor also worked tirelessly for justice and reparations for harms done to herself and others, including suing Bayer Pharmaceutical Company for their participation in the human experiments at the camps. Her work resulted in the establishment of a $5 billion Remembrance, Responsibility and Future Foundation.

We forgive people, not acts. Jasmine Syedullah, queer Black feminist, political theorist, and author, writes about the need for both personal and societal transformation. Referring to our work in societal change, she writes, "We have to balance that with the work of overthrowing the oppressive system operation internally that actually keeps us enslaved."[58] Then we can engage in the work of social justice from a place of principled love, able to hold the complexities of demanding societal transformation while living with joy, despite it all.

This is not a linear process. We don't attend our own healing and *then* engage with the world; it happens simultaneously. However, if we are to stop transmitting our own pain, we must engage in personal healing *as* we engage with the world.

And yet, if we remain siloed or stuck only in our own personal healing, we live unliberated in other ways. Life is about more than our own pain and our own healing.

As we heal and are freed from our pain, we cannot help but want that for others. It is that frame of reference in which we use our agency and help make God, or love, visible in the form of justice or collective liberation.

What is the role of the church?

What is the role of the church, and specifically our church, in issues of personal and societal liberation? I look to Rev. Dr. Martin Luther King, Jr. for the answer. In his last book, published in 1967 before his assassination, King wrote:

> Among the forces of white liberalism the church has a special obligation. It is the voice of moral and spiritual authority on earth...It has too often blessed a status quo that needed to be blasted and reassured a social order that needed to be reformed.[59]

> This is the pressing challenge confronting the white liberal. When evil men plot, good men must plan. When evil men burn and bomb, good men must build and bind. When evil men conspire to preserve an unjust status quo, good men must unite to bring about the birth of a society undergirded by justice. Nothing can be more detrimental to the health of America at this time than for liberals to sink into a state of apathy and indifference...[60]

King is clear in his call to white liberal churches and its members: We must tell the truth of our complicity, our failings, and our weaknesses, not to brand our foreheads "sinner," but to set ourselves and those we have failed—in this case Black people—free.

We witnessed the beginning of this here last Sunday when Frank Cousins, our guest and a member of a longtime Black family in Newburyport, told his father's story during the service. We heard more stories during coffee hour after the service. There has been talk on our FRSUU Members and Friends Facebook page of our engaging with the work of compiling the history of Black people in this area and in our church.

Truth-telling is essential for healing and reparations. Ibram Kendi, author, professor, and historian of race and discriminatory policy in the United States, says, "The heartbeat of racism is denial, and the heartbeat of antiracism is confession." Truth-telling isn't the end of the work, but it is an essential beginning.[61]

When Reverend Karlene Griffiths Sekou came in 2019 to help us begin our work as an antiracist congregation, she told us that the place to begin this work was by sharing our personal experiences. "Learn your own stories and let them be known," she said.

We can do this work with conviction and love, channeling our anger to fuel our commitment to and energy for the work. Personal and societal restorative work will alchemize our anger and fear and transform it into creativity, imagination, and healing so that we do not transmit the pain of this gener-ation or the past onto our children and grandchildren.

The church's role is to support and nurture personal healing *and* engage in the work of societal justice. We have committed to both of these things in our values, mission, and ends. *To care for one another. To steward history. To partner with others working for justice.*

This is real work, and it is hard work. It is messy, imperfect, and challenging, as much as it is freeing, joyful, and meaningful. It will not be completed this year or next or in our lifetimes. It is the work of lifetimes. But what more important work is there?

21
What's a Man to Do?

March 19. 2023

This sermon is dedicated to the men from the FRS Men's Group who asked me "What's a man to do?" in the 21st century. I thought long and hard about the answer to their question and have boiled my response down to three points.

What's a man to do?

   1. *Do your own work.*

This includes growing in self-awareness, which means learning how to apprentice sorrow, process grief, and forgive others and yourself. Your work as men includes being a part of a trusted community that supports you in healing your family of origin's wounds, discovering your blind spots, and developing new skills that your emotions and heart can offer.

Your work also includes recognizing the expectations and norms you were given as a male in our society and realizing how some of the things you were taught can hurt other people. Learn how to process and transform your own rage, so you don't transmit it. Then help others transform their rage. "May every one of us become more curious and less frightened of rage,"[62] says Buddhist author Ruth King.

Learn about the strength that comes from vulnerability and the power that comes from collaboration. *Do your own work...*

2. Stay true to who you truly are, underneath the expectations, burdens, and privileges of traditional manhood.

Bring your true self into the world. Don't let cynicism or fear keep you away. Debunk the myth of being "too old" or "over the hill," both of which could interfere with your work. Michael Schwalbe, North Carolina State University Professor of Sociology, writes in *The Hazards of Manhood,*

> Most American men know perfectly well the qualities they must display to be considered fully credible as men: power, competitiveness, and toughness. This turns out to be enormously useful for generating profit. Just give men opportunities to display manhood in these ways, and they'll do things that add to the bottom line, even if it's to their own detriment.[63]

Question what you've been told and drop what doesn't work. Be who *you truly are*. Who you are matters. A lot. *Stay true to who you are...*

And:

3. Listen to and help women and other traditionally marginalized people.

As a man you have irrefutable power, even if you are older than sixty-five. You have power by virtue of being a man, even if you don't have a job. You still must evaluate and change how you use or abuse the power you are granted, even if you like women and you don't believe in patriarchal values. What you believe matters; how you act and use your power matters more.

Women know about male power. *"Many of our foundational myths are, in this way, stories about men, related to men by other men,"*[64] wrote Idrees Kahloon. I received two master's degrees, one in business and the other in theology. Most of my professors in both programs were men. The vast majority of theologians and successful business leaders we studied were men, dead and alive. As a female, I was taught the same things men were taught about their power. I have also been harmed by men abusing their power in micro and macro ways.

Are you willing to learn from women?

Olympic soccer player Abby Wambach writes about a feminine understanding of power in her book, *WOLFPACK*:

> The picture of leadership is not just a man at the head of a table.
>
> It's also every woman who is allowing her own voice to guide her life and the lives of those she cares about.
>
> Leadership is volunteering at the local school, speaking encouraging words to a friend, and holding the hand of a dying parent.
>
> It's tying dirty shoelaces and going to therapy and

saying to our families and friends: No. We don't do unkindness here.

It's signing up to run for the school board and it's driving that single mom's kids home from practice and it's creating boundaries that prove to the world that you value yourself.

Leadership is taking care of yourself and empowering others to do the same.

Leadership is not a position to earn, it's an inherent power to claim.

Leadership is the blood that runs through your veins—it's born in you.

It's not the privilege of a few, it is the right and responsibility of all.

Leader is not a title that the world gives to you—

It's an offering that you give to the world.[65]

Act on behalf of women.

When the scandal with Robert Kraft visiting massage parlors in Florida was made public, I was appalled. The men I spoke to about the situation said, "People know it's wrong. We don't need to say anything." Yet *your silence is saying something,* I replied.

Men, your voices matter. They matter to me and to many women. We care that men speak out and act alongside us as we work for the rights for all women.

One in three women has been a victim of sexual abuse, including me. The number is much higher when we include other forms of physical violence. These acts of violence cannot help but affect us. Listen to and help women. Don't rescue us but be part of the solution.

You are not personally responsible for patriarchy. But there are things you can do. *Do your own work. Stay true to who you are under the expectations and burdens of manhood. Listen to and help women and other traditionally marginalized people.* All of these acts will allow men and women to be in right relationship with each other.

I'll close my answer to the question "What's a Man to Do?" with a poem by Fred LaMotte. I offer it as an invitation for men to consider as a guide for their outlooks and their actions.

Men

Men who believe women.
Men who care for women in pain.
Men who praise women when
their bodies grow old.
Men who listen to women even when
they repeat themselves.
Men who hear women even when
they do not speak.
Men who grasp whole women with their hearts,
not parts of women with their hands.
Men who hug women well, radiance to radiance.
Men who linger by forest ponds
and gaze into green stillness,

139

speaking to the great Mother.
Men who travel deep into the wilderness
not to hunt or kill,
not to climb the highest peak,
but just to be there.
Men who know valleys,
observing the etiquette of mist,
the customs of cedar and willow.
Men who understand
that the fire in their belly
is the Goddess.

Thank you for asking.

22
Room at Your Table
November 18, 2018

A parishioner recently shared with me her deepening appreciation about the importance of understanding each other and our differences. She wrote, "My awareness of the differences within humanity just keeps growing. Each of us has expanded our understanding of our world as it increasingly acknowledges and embraces differences among us."

Is that true? Is our understanding of the world expanding? Are we acknowledging and embracing differences?

It has been quite a shift for me to understand differences as something to be celebrated. As a child, I was encouraged to look for similarities between people and not to compare myself to others. Maxims of my era, social class, and race included "We're all more alike than different" and "Those who try hard enough can be anything they want to be."

It is true that there are many similarities among people. There are also amazing, beautiful, and essential differences that, when ignored, stymie us all. Denial of differences among people as it relates to class, race, and gender identity does more than thwart our development as full human beings. It fuels fear, fosters hate and prejudice, and perpetuates unjust power structures and systems. Far too often, it kills.

It is imperative that we acknowledge and celebrate our differences and create spaces and relationships where individuals are free to live in the full expression of who they truly are.

In order to do this, we welcome differences and honor the layers and complexity of people, and ourselves.

We *must* learn to live beyond a binary worldview in which people and their gender, gender identity, and sexual orientation are artificially forced into categories. This same worldview postulates that people's minds, bodies, and hearts are separate and disconnected from one another. A binary worldview requires that things and people be less complex than they are. Binary thinking suggests that something or someone is *this or that, man or woman, heterosexual or homosexual.* Those perspectives are as outdated as a Thanksgiving dinner with only turkey and no vegetarian options.

Sam Killermann's TED talk, entitled "Understanding the Complexities of Gender," captures these ideas well. He says:

> Take all people and divide them into two. Boys line up on the left; girls line up on the right. Boys, let's start with you.
>
> Boys are aggressive, impetuous, good at math, love the color blue. They get dirty, rough house, play sports but not house. Trucks and soldiers and Legos are their

142

toys, but they break them all, because boys will be boys.

Boys can grow up and be whatever they want.

The world is their oyster, and whether or not they realize it, it is their privilege to capitalize on this prize that is limited just to guys, it's there for them—the Y chromosome prize.

Girls, on the other hand, are docile, passive, natural caretakers, love the color pink, born to be good bakers. Girls hate bugs, love hugs, and are better at vacuuming rugs. Dolls and purses and makeup make their days.

While boys play with video games, girls would rather play with hair spray.

Girls grow up to be moms and leave the other jobs to dads, unless they want to be a teacher, a nurse, a receptionist, or a clerk.

What I just described certainly applies to a few of you. Yes, there are people for which these descriptions end up being true. The problem here is options, and if you're counting, we have only two.

Two options to describe every person in this room, each and every one of you. Two options to describe every person in this world. Seven billion individual different identities simplified into two. Now as you can probably guess gender isn't really that simple, it's true. In fact, there are as many versions of gender as there are number of you.[66]

Gender and sex are not the same thing. They are related, but one does not dictate the other. Sex is assigned at birth, and for 1 in 2,000 births that decision is not clear. A doctor often makes the decision in cases of gender uncertainty or intersex.

Gender Spectrum, a nonprofit dedicated to creating a gender-inclusive world for all children and youth, says that gender is the complex interrelationship between three dimensions: our body, identity, and expression. They define gender identity as "our deeply held internal sense of self as male, female, a blend of both, or neither, who we internally know ourselves to be..." and define expression as "...how we present our gender in the world and how society, culture, community, and family perceive, interact with, and try to shape our gender."[67] Gender identity and gender expression, and how they interact with each other, is as varied as there are people in the world.

Killermann tells us that gender is *not* universal or cross-cultural. Gender *is* relative, cultural, and changes over time. It is rooted in norms and is a way to classify personalities.

I was in 10th grade when my classmates and I took the "human sexuality" class. In this class, we learned about homo-sexuals, transvestites, and cross-dressers. It was right on the cusp of the use of the term transgender, and even then, this term referred to all gender non-conforming people. There was no such thing as the Genderbread Person, which our youth are introduced to in OWL. The Genderbread Person is an easy-to-understand presentation of the gender continuum. It looks at gender identity, expression, physical sex, and sexual and romantic attraction all on a continuum.[68]

The arena of LGBTQ+ issues is rapidly and continually evolving, while at the same time it is frustratingly and sadly mired in societal pushback. Change creates significant backlash, and yet, we must persist in our own evolution on these issues and in supporting societal changes that promote the rights of LGBTQ+ people.

Homosexuality was removed from the DSM as a mental illness in 1973, less than fifty years ago. It was only fourteen years ago, in 2004, that same-sex marriage become legal in our state, when Massachusetts Chief Justice Margaret Marshall stated that, "the Massachusetts Constitution affirms the dignity and equality of all individuals. It forbids the creation of second-class citizens..."[69] Same-sex marriage became fully legal in the United States only three years ago.

Lesbian, gay, bisexual, and transgender (LGBT) persons in Massachusetts have the same rights and responsibilities as heterosexuals. Just two weeks ago, the Newburyport City Council approved a resolution to uphold its commitment to defending transgender equality in the city. The resolution reaf-firms current city policy "prohibiting discrimination in places of public accommodation on the basis of gender identity and gender expression."[70]

All of this is good, and yet, there is still far to go.

FRS first became a welcoming congregation in 1996. We received re-accreditation last year and are holding this service as one of the ways that we are living into that commit-ment. The Transgender Day of Remembrance was started twenty years ago when Rita Hester, a transgender African American woman, was murdered in Allston, Massachusetts.

And there is more that we can do, as a congregation and as

individuals. I'll lift up a few things that we can consider as a congregation and then focus on us as individuals.

TRUUsT, Transgender Religious Professional Unitarian Universalists Together, founded in 2004, is a relatively new group within our faith movement dedicated to supporting trans UU religious educators and ministers. The group has a vision to grow into an organization for all trans UUs. TRUUsT has provided training for the denomination and helped trans ministers including Reverend Otto O'Connor, the first openly trans minster to serve the UU congregation in Malden, Massachusetts. That congregation's website says, "Unitarian Universalism's commitment to trans lives is all too often aspirational rather than true today. According to a recent survey, only 28% of trans UUs feel that their congregation is fully inclusive of them as trans people."[71]

TRUUsT has a list of requests for all congregations, including supporting their rapid response relief fund, hiring staff and religious professionals who are transgender, and making our communications and activities explicitly trans-friendly. There is an online course that we can all have access to as a congregation if there is interest. There are many other opportunities as well, including walking together in the North Shore Pride Walk next June.

When it comes to the individual level, we are called to make room in our minds, our hearts, and our actions. This includes making room to replace our binary thinking of gender with the reality that gender is a continuum. We can read as one way to expand our understanding from a personal level. Two great examples of that are Richard Russo's essay, "Imagining

Jenny," published in his book *The Destiny Thief*, and Janet Mock's book, *Redefining Realness*.

We can be people who speak and honor truth, putting aside what we believed to be true, and making the time and emotional room to hear each other's stories, including our own. In her book *Redefining Realness*, writer and transgender rights activist Janet Mock says, "I believe that telling our stories, first to ourselves and then to one another and the world, is a revolutionary act. It is an act that can be met with hostility, exclusion, and violence. It can also lead to love, understanding, transcendence, and community."[72]

Before we close this morning, I want to invite us all to do two things as allies of transgender people. Each of you has a slip with a name on it inside of your Order of Service. Each of these names signifies a trans person who was killed last year. In 2017 more than three hundred transgender people lost their lives to hate crimes.

Take that name and spend a moment looking at it. Take a breath, remembering that this name is a person: a person with dreams, hopes, pains, and confusion, a person who was someone's child and someone's friend. We're going to sit with this name for a minute, and then I will invite you all to speak the names that we have out loud, all together. When you leave here today, take the name with you as a reminder of their story and of our collective commitment and your personal commitment to transgender people and to peace, love, and justice. Make room at your Thanksgiving table; maybe even place the name on your table where you can remember that we are all connected.

Rather than get angry when you see that name, open your heart to compassion. Instead of feeling defeated and power-less, take one action that you can do, even reading an article or learning more. We've already lost far too many people. Let's be agents of peace, love, and compassion. We must be part of the solution. The deaths of these individuals will mean less if we lose our faith, gratitude, and open hearts. Such losses for us will make their losses only deeper. Choose well my friends. Choose love.

23

If Fear Is the Problem, What Do We Put in Its Place?

November 12, 2023

FRSUU voted to adopt the 8th Principle of Unitarian Universalism at our annual meeting in June 2024. This sermon was delivered in advance of this vote and offered my words of encouragement to move forward with this vote.

The 8th Principle

We, the member congregations of the Unitarian Universalist Association, covenant to affirm and promote: journeying toward spiritual wholeness by working to build a diverse multicultural Beloved Community by our actions that accountably dismantle racism and other oppressions in ourselves and our institutions.[73]

Hundreds of congregations across the country have adopted this principle, adding it to the current seven principles which Unitarian Universalists seek to promote: the inherent worth and dignity of all people, the interconnected web of life,

149

democracy, and the free and responsible search for truth and meaning.

"No more education or pontification about the importance of being antiracist." I thought to myself as I prepared this sermon. "Enough."

The world is at war again. Innocent civilians are being killed in mass shootings, elders and disabled people can't afford to live in our city. It is time to name what is happening in ourselves, between us, and in the world. We know we don't agree with oppression of any kind. When we hurt anyone, we hurt ourselves. When we do not care for the planet, we are not caring for ourselves or our grandchildren.

Oppression: an inequitable distribution of resources and systems that privileges some people over others and perpetuates the lies that we are not interconnected, or that violence is the answer. Oppression of any type is simply wrong.

It is misaligned with our other liberal religious values and morality. Oppression is killing our planet and far too many people, and has been doing so for a very long time. Policies of oppression may be at a heightened level right now, but this way of living is not new. What is there to dispute? Oppression and violence are not working.

As I held this knowing in my mind, body, and heart, I knew what this sermon would be about: It's about naming the fear that runs this world and our lives, asking all of us to choose differently and replace it with what we need and want, and living with and creating in the world a beloved community.

People act out, against themselves and others, when they are afraid. When they feel powerless, and unable to see a way through, they turn to the answer that they have been taught: fighting, demonizing, and *otherizing* people. From a place of fear, people separate themselves from what and who is "other." Yet spiritual masters have told us for thousands of years, and science affirms, that everything is interconnected. There is no "other." What we do to one, we do to all. When one community of people, one race, or one country suffers, we all suffer.

Fear and its close friend, anger, have reached epidemic proportions. These emotions and mindsets are stored in our bodies, passed on through generations, and in some ways so normalized that we forget, or don't realize, that there is another way.

There is another way. It is the way of peace, love, and justice: the paths that honor the interconnectedness of our world and understand deeply how *everything* that we do to another person or the Earth, we also do to ourselves. When we love another, we love ourselves. When we fear another, we fear ourselves. When we hurt another, we are hurt.

This is not rhetoric.

The replacement for fear and anger is what the Reverend Dr. Martin Luther King, Jr. called the *Beloved Community*, words used in the 8th Principle. The concept of Beloved Community is credited as originating with philosopher Josiah Royce as a "global vision of world peace put into practice by embracing the philosophy of nonviolence and reconciliation."[74] I believe there were a few great spiritual teachers before the 1800s who also taught about the way of peace, and the Beloved Community.

In Dr. King's teaching, there were six essential principles necessary to create and sustain the Beloved Community. These include:

1. All can share in the wealth of the earth.
2. International standards of human decency will protect against poverty, hunger, and homelessness.
3. An all-inclusive spirit of sisterhood and brotherhood will replace all forms of racism, discrimination, bigotry, and prejudice.
4. International disputes will be resolved by peaceful conflict-resolution and reconciliation between adversaries, instead of military power.
5. Love and trust will triumph over fear and hatred.
6. Peace and justice will prevail over war and military conflict.[75]

King placed great faith in the need for and power of reconciliation as a pathway to Beloved Community. He was no fool with respect to how violence destroys entire communities and races. Yet he said, "The end is reconciliation; the end is redemption; the end is the creation of the Beloved Community. It is this... which will bring about miracles in the hearts of men."[76]

King knew that goodwill was not enough to bring about this change of society and relations among people. He called on the power of *agape love*—love for all— "... love, which is purely spontaneous, unmotivated, groundless, and creative...love seeking to preserve and create community."[77]

This kind of love, care, and identification with our fellow humans demands that we hold a concern for all sentient beings, and all people, regardless of their beliefs, abilities, skin color, or religion. King said, "...it is...a call for an all-embracing and unconditional love for all... This often misunderstood and misinterpreted concept has now become an absolute necessity for the survival of man. When I speak of love, I am speaking of that force which all the great religions have seen as the supreme unifying principle of life."[78]

You might be thinking that these are lofty ideals, far out of reach, and not much use now. My friends, that's what values and virtues are: *ideals*. If we are not striving for our ideals and living a value-based life, then what are we striving for and what is steering our lives? How do we know how to respond if we aren't clear about the values we hold most highly?

Now is the time for pivoting and practicing new and different ways of understanding and relating to others, approaching conflict, and caring for all sentient beings who share this Earth. The time for lengthy debates or taking huge amounts of time to discern simple truths is over, at least for the time being. It's back to basics, many basics which have never been given a fair trial. Love, justice, peace, equity, honoring interconnectedness, living in Beloved Community.

We know that peace must be the answer. Oppression of any kind must come to an end. Recognition of the interconnectedness of all of life, and responding to that truth, must be the way of life and must be sustained.

If fear is the problem—and I believe that underneath everything, it is—then connection, agape love, and care for one another is the answer. Let us hold one another in great care, provide safety from a turbulent and over-whelming world, and work together for peace. Let us affirm and work toward the Beloved Community, richer for our diversity, grounded in equality, and uplifting for all.

May it be so.

Part Six

An Invitation

24
An Invitation

At a time when going to church has become less common and people are dying of loneliness, we need one another. We need to be with people who remind us what matters in life and who will work with us to do all we can to bring light and love into this world.

The First Religious Society Unitarian Universalist, its members and friends, and the communities of which we are a part, give fresh meaning to the word *hope*. We are an unusual, and at the same time, very ordinary town with hearts and minds committed to love, peace, and justice.

May we all find our way to be agents of love in this troubled and beautiful world. May we share our stories as an act of courageous love, healing and learning from each other as we do. May we listen to one another, the Earth and her creatures, and may we share in the work of collective liberation. May we move in joy and reach out in kindness while moving forward in bravery and real love, together.

Join me.

25

To Hear and Be Heard

September 30, 2018

I want to start off today's sermon by saying "Thank you." Thank you to all of you: those of you who have been coming for years, those of you who have been coming each week of my first month here, and those for whom this may be your first or second visit.

Thank you for being interested, committed, or simply willing, to be part of the story that is happening, right now, today, and this month. It is the story of a nearly 300-year-old congregation, which has called its first female minister. It is the story about community: a story about a church where people feel accepted and have meaningful relationships, and want to grow in diversity, use our resources for good, and be a part of the wider community. A story of people who are believers in hope and are invested in the outcome of what we do together. We are a people who see a future that embraces the past and who are open to the new.

I sent out a request last week via flyers, email, and Facebook, asking you all three questions:

1. Why are you a part of this church community?
2. What about FRS do you hope never changes, and why?
3. If your dreams come true, how will FRS look in five years?

Thirty-five of you, or eight percent of the 437 members, replied. Not bad for a three-day turnaround, for something not spoken of from the pulpit. The people who answered ranged from those who had just come this past month to those who have been members for seven decades. This simple—and, I'll confess, somewhat last-minute—idea has turned out to be a huge gift. Every email I've received has been rich with story. Each story is precious.

I have printed each of your stories. I am holding them dear, waiting to spend more time with each one of them. Please keep sending them in. This is good and important work for us to do at the start of this year and throughout the years to come.

Six words topped the reasons that you said you come here: "community," "spiritual," "people," "place," "worship," and "feeling" (of belonging or being accepted). Not surprisingly, a very similar list describes what you hope never changes: a community of open-minded and accepting people and a church that provides people with hope and connects them to goodness.

You wrote more than twice as much about your visions and dreams for the future of FRS. You envision a church community that is diverse in our people, music styles, and worship services. You *do* love music; it was one of the most frequently cited words. You also love and care about families, children, and younger adults. You want to be more engaged in the community and responding to issues of justice. You have dreams for the Parish Hall, whether it is to be a soup kitchen or a safe place for those who need it. You want vibrant and traditional Sunday worship and alternative worship services on other days. You recognize that this will take more staff, including lay and paid ministers.

You have big dreams, and I share them. Still, you are committed to this being a church, a place of spirituality where people support one another in asking the big questions in life and come to understand religion in relevant, new, and deeper ways. You want to be sure that we uphold our liberal religious values, are welcoming to all people, and are founded on goodness and love.

This is an exciting time to be a part of this Beloved Community. New, old, questioning, wisdom bearers—we need all of our voices, all of our stories. We have only just begun.

Let me return to our theme, stories...

Stories...

"One of our problems today is that we are not well acquainted with the literature of the spirit," writes Joseph Campbell. "We're interested in the news of the day and the problems of the hour. Thus distracted, we no longer listen to those who speak of the eternal values that have to do with the centering of their lives."[79] We no longer listen to stories.

I chose this ministry theme because I believe in the power of stories. I know that we cannot become who we are meant to be without first understanding who we've been and who we are today. This is true for groups as well as individuals. We cannot change until we, at a minimum, accept what has been true and what currently is true. If we are lucky, we not only accept, but we also learn from what has been. We use our stories and experiences as teachers—guides for what matters to us and who we are called to be, again, individually and collectively.

As a spiritual community—a religious body founded on covenant or promises to principles rather than dogma or creed—we need to learn the spiritual practice of storytelling. Storytelling is a practice in that we do it again and again. As some people say, we tell our stories until they do not need to be told anymore. Storytelling is a spiritual practice because it helps us to make meaning and to connect.

We tell stories with our faith journeys as well as other parts of our lives. What a gift that there are avenues here at FRS to practice this. I'm going to highlight two ways, though there are many more.

One thing you can do is to join a Chalice Circle; these are small groups that meet monthly for the course of the church year. The groups are led by a peer facilitator. Small groups of people come together to delve deeper into issues that matter, questions of the mind and heart. The Chalice Circles this year will be seeking to include topics connected to our ministry themes including ideas such as creativity, balance, and intention. These groups are open to everyone and are a great way for new people to get to know other parishioners and for long-term people to stay connected and meet new people. Chalice Circles will be starting in October. You can sign up during coffee hour today.

Another thing you can do is to write your own Journey of Faith. We were honored to hear parishioner Vern Ellis offer his Journey of Faith this morning. This is the ninth year that we are doing this at FRS. Across the board, people talk about the transforming power of preparing their Journey of Faith. I encourage you strongly to consider signing up to do this. As an added benefit, you will receive support along the way. Who knows, I may offer a multi-session class on this if there is enough interest.

In addition to Chalice Circles and Journeys of Faith, we have a meditation group, several different book groups, and groups of folks who gather on multiple different issues of social justice. All of these are avenues to get to know others, to build community, to hear and be heard.

One might wonder why we need to practice telling stories. I mean, what is there to practice? There are many skills which we develop as we engage in the spiritual practice of story-telling including discernment, creative expression, and truth-telling. Perhaps no skill is more necessary, however, than listening. "All 'community,'" write the authors of *The Spirituality of Imperfection*, "begins in listening... What happens first in any 'community' is that those who would participate in it listen."[80]

One of the beautiful things about Chalice Circles is the prac-tice of deep listening. Akin to what happens in twelve-step recovery meetings, when a person is talking, others listen. There is no interrupting, fixing, or telling of our own similar stories. It is a profound and transformative process of bearing witness, or the ministry of presence. Easier for some of us than others, listening without *doing* anything allows the others to find their own answers or listen to their own knowing. This is a gift we can give one another here.

Philosopher and poet Mark Nepo says, "...we hear in equal measure to what we listen with. When we listen with our mind, we understand more of life. When we listen with our heart, we feel more of life. When we listen with our entire being and spirit, we are transformed and joined with life itself."[81]

Cantognake, or love, one of the twelve Lakota virtues, means, "To place and hold in one's heart." Telling stories, listening, being heard are some of the most profound ways to do this.

You may remember a study that I quoted from earlier this month, a study done at Stanford Graduate School of Business. This study found that we remember information shared in stories twenty-two times more than information we learn in other ways.[82]

Sharing with one another in this way will bind us. It will call us to stop, look, and remember—each other (as it says so beautifully on the cover of the Order of Service). It will, like the story of the Velveteen Rabbit, or my own Thumbelina, make us real. We will learn to know one another, to experience one another, and thus to love one another.

Maya Angelou said that "There is no greater agony than bearing an untold story inside you."[83] I believe this. Our stories are our lives.

One of you wrote this in response to my three questions: "I've often said to people asking about FRS that this is the church of 'living.' A deep spiritual and nurturing place that helps me live a better life." I believe that too.

We are indeed a church about living. Referring to the words of Joseph Campbell again, we are, I hope, people "who speak of the eternal values that have to do with the centering of their lives." We do this so that we continue to create a community of diversity and acceptance, so that we may understand ourselves and one another, and so that, ultimately, we can go out into the world and create peace.

Amen and Blessed Be.

Notes

1. Lily Rothman, "Margaret Atwood on Serial Fiction and the Future of the Book," *Time*, October 8, 2012, http://entertainment.time.com/2012/10/08/margaret-atwood-on-serial-fiction-and-the-future-of-the-book/.
2. Cody C. Delistraty, "The Psychological Comforts of Storytelling," *The Atlantic*, November 2, 2014, https://www.theatlantic.com/health/archive/2014/11/the-psychological-comforts-of-storytelling/381964/.
3. Delistraty, "The Psychological Comforts of Storytelling."
4. Chimamanda Ngozi Adichie, "The danger of a single story," TED Talk, July 2009, https://www.ted.com/talks/chimamanda_adichie_the_danger_of_a_single_story?language=en.
5. Mitra Rahnema, *Centering: Navigating Race, Authenticity, and Power in Ministry* (Skinner House Books, 2017), 190.

6. Delistraty, "The Psychological Comforts of Storytelling."
7. Robin Wall Kimmerer, "Speaking of Nature," *Orion Magazine*, June 12, 2017, https://orionmagazine.org/article/speaking-of-nature/.
8. Robin Wall Kimmerer, "Learning the Grammar of Animacy," *The Leopold Outlook*, Winter 2012.
9. Kimmerer, "Learning the Grammar of Animacy."
10. Kimmerer, "Learning the Grammar of Animacy."
11. David Whyte, *Everything Is Waiting for You* (Many Rivers Press, 2003).
12. John O'Donohue, *Beauty: The Invisible Embrace* (Harper Perennial, 2005).
13. Rabbi Bradley Shavit Artson, *God of Becoming and Relationship: The Dynamic Nature of Process Theology* (Jewish Light Publishing, 2016), xv-xvi.
14. C. Robert Mesle, *Process-Relational Philosophy: An Introduction to Alfred North Whitehead* (Templeton Press, 2008), 87.
15. Mesle, *Process-Relational Philosophy*, 10.
16. Artson, *God of Becoming and Relationship*, xiii.
17. Mesle, *Process-Relational Philosophy*, 37.
18. Mesle, *Process-Relational Philosophy*, 18.
19. Rebecca Solnit, *A Paradise Built in Hell: The Extraordinary Communities That Arise in Disaster* (Penguin Group, 2009), 3.
20. Denise Levertov, *The Stream & the Sapphire: Selected Poems on Religious Themes*, "The Servant-Girl at Emmaus (A Painting by Velázquez)" (New Directions, 36008th edition, May 17, 1997).
21. William Blake, "Auguries of Innocence," 1863.

22. Brené Brown, *Rising Strong: How the Ability to Reset Transforms the Way We Live, Love, Parent, and Lead* (Random House, 2017).

23. Khalil Gibran, *Sand and Foam* (Alfred A. Knopf, 1967).

24. William Murray, *A Faith for All Seasons: Liberal Religion and the Crises of Life* (River Road Press, 1990).

25. Khalil Gibran, *Sand and Foam*.

26. Francis Weller, *The Wild Edge of Sorrow: Rituals of Renewal and the Sacred Work of Grief* (North Adams Books, 2015), xix.

27. Weller, *The Wild Edge of Sorrow*, xiv.

28. Weller, *The Wild Edge of Sorrow*, xix.

29. Weller, *The Wild Edge of Sorrow*, xxii.

30. Weller, *The Wild Edge of Sorrow*, 42.

31. Weller, *The Wild Edge of Sorrow*, 58.

32. Weller, *The Wild Edge of Sorrow*, 70.

33. Weller, *The Wild Edge of Sorrow*, xxiii.

34. Weller, *The Wild Edge of Sorrow*, 126.

35. Modified from original quote changing "man" and "him" to gender-neutral language.

36. William Bridges, *Transitions: Making Sense of Life's Changes* (Da Capo Press, 2004), Kindle, location 277.

37. Bridges, *Transitions*, location 359.

38. Bridges, *Transitions*, location 359.

39. Corinna da Fonseca-Wollheim, "How the Silence Makes the Music," *The New York Times*, October 2, 2019.

40. Aldous Huxley, *Music at Night and Other Essays* (Chatto & Windus, 1931).

41. Eckhart Tolle, "What Are the Vertical and Horizontal Dimensions? Eckhart Tolle on Awareness," YouTube,

August 3, 2023, https://youtu.be/hGB9tfmhVA8?si=SoEDEo1u0SUddoZk.

42. Sonali Bansal, "Axis Mundi–Understanding the Connection Between Heaven & Hell," Fractal Enlightenment, https://fractalenlightenment.com/35796/spirituality/axis-mundi-understanding-the-connection-between-heaven-hell.

43. Bansal, "Axis Mundi."

44. Oscar Arias Sánchez, Nobel Peace Prize Acceptance Speech, The Nobel Prize, December 10, 1987, https://www.nobelprize.org/prizes/peace/1987/arias/acceptance-speech/#:~:text=Peace%20is%20not%20a%20matter,many%20people%20in%20many%20countries.

45. Scott W. Alexander, "Getting Serious About Unitarian Universalism," Unitarian Universalist Association, posted January 21, 2015, https://www.uua.org/worship/words/sermon/183412.shtml.

46. Eric Schaal, "Which Beatles Album Sold the Most Copies All-Time?" Showbiz CheatSheet, February 27, 2019, https://www.cheatsheet.com/entertainment/which-beatles-album-sold-the-most-copies-all-time.html/.

47. Jordan Runtagh, "Beatles' 'Sgt. Pepper' at 50: When Jesus Dropped by During 'Fixing a Hole' Sessions," *Rolling Stone*, May 22, 2017, https://www.rollingstone.com/music/music-features/beatles-sgt-pepper-at-50-when-jesus-dropped-by-during-fixing-a-hole-sessions-122996/.

48. Amanda Gorman, "Practice Makes People," in *Call Us What We Carry: Poems* (Viking Books, 2021).

49. Steven Johnson, *The Invention of Air: A Story of Science, Faith, Revolution, and the Birth of America* (Riverhead Books, 2008).

50. "7th Principle: Respect for the Interdependent Web of All Existence of Which We Are a Part," Unitarian Universalist Association, accessed December 2018, https://www.uua.org/beliefs/what-we-believe/principles/7th.

51. Johnson, *The Invention of Air*, xviii.

52. Johnson, *The Invention of Air*, 17.

53. Johnson, *The Invention of Air*, 57.

54. Johnson, *The Invention of Air*, 71.

55. Rev. angel Kyodo williams, Lama Rod Owens, and Jasmine Syedullah, *Radical Dharma: Talking Race, Love, and Liberation* (North Atlantic Books, 2016), 39.

56. williams, Owens, and Syedullah, *Radical Dharma*, Editor's note.

57. "Eva Kor," The Forgiveness Project, accessed January 2021, https://www.theforgivenessproject.com/stories/eva-kor/.

58. williams, Owens, and Syedullah, *Radical Dharma*, 54.

59. Martin Luther King, Jr., *Where Do We Go from Here: Chaos or Community?* (Beacon Press, 1968), 101-102.

60. King, *Where Do We Go from Here*, 94.

61. Ibram Kendi, "The difference between being 'not racist' and antiracist," TED, May 2020, https://www.ted.com/talks/ibram_x_kendi_the_difference_between_being_not_racist_and_antiracist?utm_campaign=tedspread&utm_medium=referral&utm_source=tedcomshare.

62. Ruth King, *Healing Rage: Women Making Inner Peace Possible* (Gotham Books, 2007).

63. Michael Schwalbe, "The Hazards of Manhood," *Yes Magazine*, Fall 2012, 42.

64. Idrees Kahloon, "What's the Matter with Men?," *The New Yorker*, January 30, 2023, 3.

65. Abby Wambach, *WOLFPACK: How to Come Together, Unleash our Power, and Change the Game* (Celadon Books, 2019), 40-41.

66. Sam Killermann, "Understanding the Complexities of Gender," May 2013 at TEDxUofIChicago, video, https://www.samkillermann.com/work/ted-x-talk-understanding-the-complexities-of-gender/.

67. https://www.genderspectrum.org/.

68. Sam Killerman, "The Genderbread Person version 4," http://itspronouncedmetrosexual.com/2018/10/the-genderbread-person-v4/

69. Jerome Pohlen, *Gay & Lesbian History for Kids: The Century-Long Struggle for LGBT Rights* (Review Press, 2016), 137-139.

70. Jack Shea, "Newburyport City Council adopts transgender equality resolution," *The Daily News*, October 31, 2018, https://www.newburyportnews.com/news/local_news/newburyport-city-council-adopts-transgender-equality-resolution/article_fe6aef77-b35b-5746-a33f-9416f8432563.html.

71. "TRUUsT Releases Unprecedented Report on Trans UUs," Unitarian Universalist Association, February 5, 2019, https://www.uua.org/midamerica/news/blog/truust-releases-unprecedented-report-trans-uus. [Ed. Note: the webpage linked with the original URL, https://transuu.org/about/, no longer lists the survey information.]

72. Janet Mock, *Redefining Realness: My Path to Womanhood, Identity, Love & So Much More* (Atria Books, Reprint edition, 2014).

73. The 8th Principle of Unitarian Universalism, https://www.8thprincipleuu.org/.

74. *The Stanford Encyclopedia of Philosophy*, The Metaphysics Research Lab, Department of Philosophy, Stanford University, https://plato.stanford.edu/entries/royce/.

75. "The Beloved Community," Module 3-Unit 3-Lesson Plan 1, Grades 6-12, https://thekingcenter.org/lesson/the-beloved-community/.

76. "The Beloved Community."

77. "The Beloved Community."

78. "The Beloved Community."

79. Ernest Kurtz and Katherine Ketcham, *The Spirituality of Imperfection: Storytelling and the Search for Meaning* (Bantam Books, 1992/2002), 8.

80. Kurtz and Ketcham, *The Spirituality of Imperfection*, 95.

81. Mark Nepo, *Seven Thousand Ways to Listen: Staying Close to What is Sacred* (Atria Books, 2012), 88.

82. Delistraty, "The Psychological Comforts of Storytelling"; Jennifer Aaker, "Harnessing the Power of Stories," Stanford Graduate School of Business, https://leanin.org/education/harnessing-the-power-of-stories.

83. Maya Angelou, *I Know Why the Caged Bird Sings* (Ballantine Books, Reissue edition, 2009).

Acknowledgments

This book was made possible with the support of many people, including all the members and friends of the First Religious Society Unitarian Universalist in Newburyport, Massachusetts. Ours is a shared ministry committed to love, peace, and justice.

Thank you to all my mentors who supported my path to ministry: Terasa Cooley, who first told me she wanted to hear what I had to say, Katie Lee Crane, Carolyn Patierno, John Gibbons, and many other amazing colleagues. Thank you to my spiritual guides, Marye Gail Harrison, Cruger Phillips, and Deb Bertges, who have been with me every step of the way.

A special thanks to John Mercer, who helped to facilitate my match with FRSUU, was an irreplaceable supporter, and edited many sermons. Thank you from the bottom of my heart to Diane Forman and Diane Carroll, who made this book possible. Diane Forman, thank you for telling me how important it was to write this book and helping bring it to fruition. As my editor, you have been a minister's and writer's mensch. Diane Carroll, you are an essential partner in my ministry. Thank you for your attention to detail and care for every person at FRSUU, along with your steady help and support, both in proofreading and organizing this book, and ensuring that all church administration tasks are completed stupendously. Many thanks also to Lance Hidy, who so beautifully designed the book covers, and to Matthew Muise whose photography blesses my life.

And, of course, deep thanks to my family: Bart, Ginger, and Jacob, who have witnessed the behind the scenes of my ministry and never wavered in their support and belief in the messages within this book.

I love you all.